UNDER THE INFLUENCE

UNDER THE INFLUENCE

Pastor Dr. Raab.
Enjoyed
being at your
church. You are
a great speaker
Phil Hamman
5-4-14

PHIL HAMMAN

eLectio Publishing

Little Elm, TX

www.eLectioPublishing.com

Table of Contents

PART TWO: MY STRUGGLE

PART THREE: MY REFORMATION

PART FOUR: MY AWARENESS

Prologue

I never had plans to share any of these stories. It started out as a way to stimulate the interest of high school students, to encourage them to write personal narratives in the Contemporary Literature class where I teach high school. The co-teacher working with me was moved by a couple of the stories and encouraged me to write more and more. I hope that by reading this, people see that there is hope when they live in a dysfunctional situation; that they can overcome adversity; and most importantly that they can make positive changes to who they are. This is the account of my life, and all of the people and events are real. Only a few names have been changed to protect the privacy of those people. I don't always write in chronological order, but rather tell about events that connect the characters so that the stories flow together. How I wish that so many of these stories were not true. Writing some of this was very difficult for me as it opened up events in my life that I had worked hard to forget and block from my memory. My family said my personality was altered while writing this as I sometimes grew edgy and short tempered. The reason I didn't tell these stories for years is that I was ashamed of my childhood, I'm embarrassed now of many things I did in my past, and I'm not proud to share some of these situations. Growing up as I did many of the things I was doing wrong seemed normal, and it took me many years to change my behaviors. But I think there's a message to be learned from these stories which can only come from me being completely frank. I now realize my life has been like a difficult labor during childbirth. In the beginning it is long and painful, but when it's over and the wounds heal, the resulting new life is a sight to behold.

For the people in my life, above all, I write this with the greatest respect for my wife, Sandy. Her total commitment to our family and her loving, patient ways helped keep me on the path. To Jordan and Angela, my love for you knows no limits. To those very important people I talk about in this story, thank you for showing me the way to set goals, work hard, and to see the possibility of a functional life beyond the Norton-Froehlich Addition.

PART ONE

MY ROOTS

Ephesians 6:4a

*"Fathers, do not provoke your children to anger
by the way you treat them." (NLT)*

Mean Streets

The day was hot and humid, one of those days when you can smell the tar from the road as it bakes in the sun. Smoke from garbage incinerators lingered in the stale air. I walked down the street of my neighborhood shirtless but wearing a pair of long blue jeans; the sun's heat beat down on my tanned back and shoulders. I was on my way to a friend's house when a group of five kids came out of nowhere. They were all from my neighborhood and had me surrounded before I could even think. Fear instantly racked my body since these kids were at least four years older than I was, and I knew them to be mean bullies. They closed their circle tighter around me and began taking turns hitting and kicking me. I knew by experience to not show how frightened I felt. Fear showed weakness, and the bullies from my neighborhood would only be encouraged by tears or cowardice. Nothing would have given them more pleasure than to exploit weakness.

"Cry for us, and we'll let you run home," one of the kids taunted.

I refused to cry and give them the satisfaction so the physical abuse continued. Not satisfied with just beating me, this group of kids knocked me to the ground and took hold of my legs. They pulled me to edge of the street where pieces of a pop bottle were shattered in the road. I held my breath trying to think of ways to protect myself, but there was nothing I could do. I felt the abrasive road on my bare back as they pulled me toward the pile of glass. They began dragging my shirtless body back and forth over the top of the broken glass. It felt like a swarm of hornets stinging me as the razor sharp shards cut into my flesh. When they saw blood pooling in the street, they ran off finally leaving me alone. I can still remember the strong smell of blood and seeing it run down my arms and legs, the sight which finally caused me to break down and cry.

I was taken to the hospital for multiple stitches. Two of those kids were sent to the state training school in Plankinton, South Dakota for this incident.

When people envision a place where crazy, often violent incidents occur, they tend to think of big cities like Chicago, L.A., or a housing project in some other big city ghetto, yet I grew up in the heartland of our country. Sioux Falls, South Dakota is where I was born and raised, an unlikely setting for the background of my stories. The neighborhood I grew up in was the Norton-Froehlich housing addition.

In the 1950's, when our country was deescalating the army bases around the nation, someone got the idea to not destroy these out-of-commission barracks. The Norton-Froehlich Addition was comprised of tiny homes and these old army barracks which had been chopped down into housing units for very low-income families. Let me explain what these barracks and Norton-Froehlich were like: we called it our house, but it was really more like a shack. Many units, including ours, didn't even have shingles, but rather tar paper stapled to the roof. The houses were about 10 feet wide by 25 feet long. Each had a small kitchen, two small bedrooms, and a tiny cubicle bathroom with an indoor toilet, very small sink, and tiny bathtub. The only heat source was a fuel oil stove in the middle of a very small living room. It was the equivalent of a pot-belly stove as it had to heat the whole place without the benefit of heat vents or registers. Our only water source was well water, which was often discolored and had a foul odor. Around the barracks lay junk automobiles, dirty trash piles with rusty beer cans, old moldy newspapers, and empty motor oil cans were strewn about. The yards were un-cut and overgrown with thistles and weeds. Yellow dandelions dotted the weed patches. Some people made feeble efforts to make the area look homey by painting their front doors in bright colors and putting flower pots on the steps. But these improvements did little to enhance the gloomy surroundings. Most of these efforts looked out of place. In every yard there was a clothes line with tattered clothes flapping in the breeze. Little children played in yards or in the street. Most were barefoot with matted, uncombed hair. Their grimy faces were caked with dirt. They saw their world through sad, hopeless eyes.

I suppose turning these barracks into living quarters sounded like a good idea, but it turned out to be a breeding ground for crime and violence. If you read the definition for *dysfunctional*, it would probably come pretty close to describing my neighborhood and the people I grew up around. Some of the Norton-Froehlich residents were just functional enough to fill out the forms to get a low-income housing unit but not functional enough to follow through with even getting shingles for the roof. It was just easier to staple tar paper to the roof. One of my neighbors scraped together the money to buy a spider monkey that rode around on his kids' backs and took baths with them yet they hardly ever had food in the house.

We had all kinds of nuts, including Crazy Clay down the street who walked around his yard in just underwear, and who had a standoff with the cops. One night he decided to just go outside and start blasting his firearm into the air until he was eventually surrounded by deputy sheriffs. After many hours they were able to take him away for a little 'vacation' that included quiet time and medication. He came back, though. You made sure you didn't walk by his place at night. Crazy Clay died one day when he blew his house off the foundation, and blew himself up trying to improperly light his propane furnace. Bullying was rampant in Norton-Froehlich, and I saw the ugly side of human nature every day. I learned not to trust anyone and became angry and violent myself. I also became misanthropic for a long time, allowing myself only a select few people to be somewhat close to. Walking down the streets of Norton-Froehlich when the weather was nice and windows were open, anyone could hear the sounds of violence spilling out onto the street. Women were frequently the recipients of abuse, and it took me many years to learn how to treat a woman with respect. The sound of a woman being beaten was a common occurrence growing up.

These photos represent all that is left of the Norton-Froehlich housing units from when I grew up.

Note how small the house is in comparison with the home and double garage of average size built next to it.

Note the vent stack for the fuel oil stove.

Note the tar paper roof

Early Life

My dad was a violent drunk who took delight in beating my mom, two older sisters, and me. He would frequently disappear and be gone on two or three day drunks. Several times while eating supper, my dad, in a violent rage, would jump up from his chair during an argument with my mom and tip the whole table over. All the food, plates, and utensils would be strewn across the floor, now mingled with broken glass. I recall one time he did this and made us all sit on the floor and keep eating the dirty food right off the floor. Many times he grabbed my mom by the hair, snatched a butcher knife off the table, and put her up against the wall with the knife held across her throat threatening to slit her open. I sat glued to my chair certain that this would be the time he'd actually do it. I knew he was going to kill her; it was only a matter of when. I developed stomach problems as a child, likely as a result of being exposed to all the stress. I also had a bad temper, and my mom and aunts would grab me and tell me I was going to end up in prison.

I know now that my dad was also a sadist. I recall he had two coon hounds that he wanted to get blood thirsty. One night he brought home a cute little baby raccoon and let us play with it. I wanted to keep it for a pet. That very night, after my dad had begun drinking, he said, "I'll show you what baby coons are good for." He took hold of the baby coon by the scruff of its neck with one hand and in the other hand he held a pair of pliers. With the baby coon screaming in pain he busted off all its teeth with the pliers so that it couldn't bite his coon hounds. Then he made me watch while he threw the baby raccoon to the dogs where it was torn apart. That night I cried myself to sleep.

I was the youngest, and my two older sisters were four and five years older than I was. When I was about six years old I can remember my dad calling home drunk late at night and telling my mom he was going to come home and kill her. She would get us kids out of bed, and I knew what the routine would be. She would put us in her car and park in the dark a ways down from our house. Before long my dad would drive to our place and stagger into the house. After what seemed to be an eternity, my mom would tell my sisters to go and make sure he was passed out. My sisters would scout the place and come back to the car to confirm that he was passed out. Then we'd all tip toe quietly back into our place so as not to wake him. Unfortunately, sometimes he would wake up and one or more of us would be beaten.

People will wonder why my mom didn't call the sheriff. I remember that she did call and the sheriff would say, "This is a family matter, and there's nothing we can really do about private family problems." This was in the days before domestic violence laws and safe houses for women. Believe me, my mom paid dearly at the hands of my dad for those calls to the sheriff after he left.

Why didn't my mom leave him? I now know my mom was co-dependent and couldn't pull away. She was born one of seven children who grew up in the Great Depression. Her father hung himself when he couldn't provide for his family after trying to work at the John Morrell packing house as a "scab" during a union strike. My mom's older brother had to go out to the barn to cut him down from the rafters. They were left to fend for themselves, and my mom was often sent to go behind the grocery store to see if there was any salvageable food in the dumpster.

Psychologically, my mom was stuck in this dysfunctional cycle. So, the abuse continued. I don't think my mom ever had the same pair of eye glasses for more than a couple of months. My dad was always punching her in the face, and her glasses were constantly being broken. When my mom and sisters were getting violently beaten I often contemplated shooting him. I damn near did shoot him one night, and I even had the shotgun loaded but froze and couldn't carry out the task. I remember feeling weak and guilty that I didn't kill him to save my mom and sisters. We were all oppressed by his violent, unpredictable behavior.

Becoming Tough

In my neighborhood you had to learn to become hard, and you had to learn how to fight. In fact, the adults encouraged fist fights and would even show up to watch their kids in a street fight. When I was in high school, I got into a big dispute with a co-worker who was my age regarding job assignments. This kid's family knew the boss very well, so my boss took his side. I told my boss he could shove the job because I was quitting. This co-worker thought it was funny and laughed about it, so I told him that when he got off work I'd be waiting for him and then he could see how funny it was. I called my mom and told her what had transpired and that I was going to wait for this kid and kick his ass. My mom said, "I'm going to stop and get a thermos of coffee and come down to watch. Don't beat him up until I get there." Not exactly the finest example of parenting. My earliest memory of fist fighting occurred at Drake Springs Swimming Pool. I couldn't have been more than five or six years old.

There, my sisters arranged a fight that was one of those 'my little brother is tougher than your brother' fights. A crowd of kids brought the other young kid and me to a phone booth on the street corner and put us both inside the booth so we couldn't run away. In my mind, I can still see all those faces pressed up against the glass of the phone booth yelling and encouraging us to keep fighting.

I don't know how long that fight lasted or who even won. I do remember being toe-to-toe with that other kid and just punching and kicking until I was exhausted. After the fight, I recall the taste of blood in my mouth and older kids telling me I was a tough kid. That tough kid mentality hung with me for far too many years, which led to personal problems and legal trouble.

Redneck Reunions

On the Fourth of July, we would go to a small town in Minnesota for our annual family reunion, and all of our hillbilly relatives would show up. The reunion was held at the home of our cousin who owned a junkyard with about 200 junked automobiles. While the adults drank, the kids played in the junkyard and shot firecrackers. Gunpowder smoke from the bottle rockets and firecrackers hung in the air all day long. Someone got burned every year on fireworks, and we were always getting hurt in that junkyard on the broken glass and sharp, jagged chrome. Every year, one of the kids had to go to the hospital for stitches. One 4th of July my cousin was sliding off the back of a junk car and cut her 'tootie.' 'Tootie' was the word we used for private parts. She had to go to the emergency room and get stitches on her tootie. After that we could get her fighting mad by taunting her with, "You tore your tootie!" But we were never stopped from playing in the junkyard.

One time our cousin Curly was lost in the junkyard. He was about eight years old, and we called him Curly because he had curly hair like a girl. All the kids were playing hide-and-seek, and Curly was never found. We all just forgot about him and went in and ate. About an hour later, some adult asked, "Where is Curly?"A hunt was organized to find Curly, and one of the adults heard a pounding sound coming from a junk car. Curly was in the trunk where he had hidden during the game. It was hot, and Curly had been trapped for over two hours. He'd almost suffocated and was listless and had to be carried into the house. Incidentally, Curly grew to be 6'7" and 275 lbs. He played Division I football and made it to the first pre-season game with a professional football team before he was cut.

Another oddity is that I had three cousins named John Henry. They all had been named after a great-uncle named John Henry. So, there were four John Henrys, but two had different last names. Strange. Uncle Hank and another uncle, John (but not a John Henry!) would get very drunk at the reunions and get into fist fights in the backyard. All of us kids would stand and watch as they exchanged punches. When a punch landed you could distinctly hear the "crack" sound it produced.

Sometimes after the fight, they would both pass out together on the back lawn, and all of us kids would be told to stay away from them so they wouldn't wake up and start fighting again. A short time later, Uncle John was killed walking home. He was drunk and walking along the highway and staggered in front of a car.

All these people had to be fed, and Grandma Louise did all the cooking at every reunion. She had a recipe for fried chicken that had its own, unique flavor. She cooked big roasting pans full of chicken. I don't know how it was seasoned, and the recipe is probably lost as I've never had chicken that tasted the same since then. She made all the potatoes and potato salad as well. In an iron kettle there was gravy cooking, and on long wooden tables were platters of biscuits and dishes of oatmeal cookies. The countertops were crowded with bowls filled with hazelnuts, walnuts, and strong-smelling pickled herring. Grandma Louise was actually my second cousins' grandma rather than my grandma, but we all called her Grandma Louise. She was one of those old-time ladies left over from the pioneer days, and her cooking, which included lard cracklings, reflected that. When I was a little kid she seemed to be a hundred years old but was probably in her late 70's. Other relatives brought salads, desserts, and deviled eggs.

At one of the reunions, Grandma Louise went into the pantry to get some canned goods and came running out screaming, "There's a skunk in the pantry!"

One of the men said, "If you shoot a skunk in the head it can't release its smell."

One of the older cousins went and got a rifle and some of us kids wanted to watch. He shot the skunk, but the head shot theory turned out to be an Old Wives' Tale. The house was engulfed with skunk stink. All the doors and windows were opened, and Grandma Louise finished the cooking with a clothes pin on her nose.

Later on when we ate I gagged and felt ill because all the food tasted like skunk. Those reunions were all just another part of my crazy upbringing.

Trauma

One of my sisters was like a mother to me. She took care of me when I was sick and would even go hungry in order to give me some of her own food when there was little in the house. Once I almost died from an infected hernia, but my sister heard me moaning in the middle of the night and made arrangements to get me to the hospital. She was not only good to me but to vulnerable animals or anyone who needed help.

It was early fall, and I was coming home from a hike down by the river where I'd spent the day fishing for carp. I could hear the screaming and yelling as I approached our house, and my stomach curled into a knot wondering what was up this time. I opened the door to find my mom and dad yelling at each other and my mom crying. What really caught my attention were the blood splatters all over the linoleum floor of the kitchen. I looked my mom over and didn't see any blood on her.

"What's going on? Who's bleeding?" I yelled.

But my question was lost in the air as they continued yelling at each other. I followed the blood trail which grew in volume as I approached the bathroom. We had a very small cubical of a bathroom, and I found my sister bent over the sink with blood pooled and smeared all over the room.

"What happened? Oh No! What is wrong with you?" I asked.

When she lifted her head and turned toward me, I could see the terror in her eyes. All of her front teeth were bashed out. My dad, in a drunken rage, had beaten her with his fists, knocking them out of her mouth.

After the arguing finally stopped, she was rushed to an emergency dentist appointment. My dad said we were all to say that she fell against a cement step, and it was made clear to us what would happen if we said differently.

The deputy sheriff did show up at our house later, and I heard my dad tell him the bogus story. The deputy stood with his arms folded, staring at my dad. Anyone could tell the deputy didn't believe my dad. After the deputy stared at my dad for about 10 seconds, he just shook his head and went back to the squad car.

I can only imagine how that may have impacted her life. That poor girl should never have had to experience something that horrible. I fell into a troubled sleep that night. My stomach aches grew increasingly worse, and my anger deepened. The abuse didn't stop for any of us.

Even today when I'm deer hunting and need to follow a deer's blood trail, I can't help but think back to when I followed my sister's blood trail so many years ago.

Firearms and Dogs

Everyone seemed to have firearms, and there were numerous incidents of violence involving firearms. There were armed stand offs with the sheriff, suicides, and murder in my neighborhood. Even pets were not safe. If you had a dog, you'd better keep it on a chain or locked up so it wouldn't get shot.

I saw my dad shoot dogs on our property with the .22 rifle and then throw the bodies into our incinerator where we burned our garbage as there was no sanitation service to our area. A burning dog in the incinerator made the air smell horrible.

We had a golden Labrador named Shane whom I loved very much. One morning, Shane must have escaped his chain. I was sound asleep when a loud gunshot just outside my window made me instantly sit upright in bed. Moments later Shane starting whining and whimpering. When we all rushed outside we found Shane with his side blown out by a shotgun blast and his guts spilled out around him on the ground. He lay in a pool of blood. My dad finished him off with the .22, and we buried Shane.

We never found out who shot him, but the incident only served to deepen my hatred for mankind.

It seemed that almost everyone in our neighborhood owned a dog, some nice but most mean. It amazes me now how so many of those people couldn't afford a car or telephone but they had firearms and dogs. Many were involved in dog fighting. Three housing units down from us, the people owned a vicious dog that was half wolf and half German shepherd. Its name, coincidentally, was Shane. I guess Shane was a popular name for a dog in those days. This Shane was huge and all gray. He looked like a Timber wolf, and he was the meanest of all mean dogs. Many kids fell victim to Shane as he broke several chains and collars in his quest to attack humans. I, too, was a victim two days after Shane attacked a little six-year-old girl named Lori Lee. Lori Lee lived across from Shane's owners and was playing in her front yard when Shane broke loose. I was playing in my yard when I heard snarling, yelling, and commotion down the street. Neighbors had gathered in the yard and Shane's owner was dragging him back into the house by his collar.

I ran down to Lori Lee's house to see what was going on. The back of her leg by the hamstring was torn away and I could actually see her leg bone. The bone glistened all shiny white like the cue ball on a billiards table. Again, this was in the days before there were vicious dog laws and lawsuits against owners of vicious dogs.

The day Shane attacked me was a hot summer afternoon. Walking down the street, I could see Shane staked on a chain. When he saw me he leaped to his feet and strained against his chain, jerking and snarling in an effort to get loose. Suddenly, the stake pulled loose from the ground, and he tore down the street after me. I can hardly describe the electricity that shot through me as I frantically looked for a safe place to run to escape this attack. There were no trees close by to climb or even a parked car to jump into or onto. The best I could see was a tall chain link fence about ten yards away, but I wasn't sure I could get to it before Shane got to me. I ran faster than I ever had in my life. I reached that fence just as Shane got to me. I scrambled toward the top and was just ready to swing one leg over when Shane leaped up and sank his fangs into my butt. He hung onto my backside and yanked, trying to pull me to the ground. I clung to the fence with all my might knowing what would happen if he succeeded in pulling me to the ground. Fueled by adrenalin, I pulled with all my strength and heaved my body to the other side. I fell safely to the other side and immediately checked the damage. The rear of my pants was ripped away, and I could feel warm blood oozing down my leg.

When I got home, I looked in the mirror at the deep puncture wounds in my backside. Throwing the jeans away, I doctored the injury the best I could and didn't tell anybody as I never knew how my crazy dad would react.

One night, someone did shoot that ferocious dog, but he didn't die. His owners took him to the vet where the dog's front leg was amputated at the shoulder due to damage from the bullet. Shane could still move quickly on three legs, though. That dog continued to be the fiercest three-legged dog that ever lived.

A Good Dog?

Just down the street from us lived some neighbors who owned a German shepherd named Teddy. Teddy was black and tan and looked just like the famous dog on TV, Rin Tin Tin. He was protective of his family and those he considered worthy of protection, which happened to include me for some reason. When I was about 6 years old, I'd go and play with Teddy in his yard. I could pet him or hang on him and he was never mean or frightening. Teddy's owners kept a large water trough in the backyard which was filled with water so their kids could play in it like a small swimming pool. I would take all my clothes off and play in the water trough.

One afternoon while I was splashing away without a care in the world, my mom drove by and saw me in the trough with no clothes on. She got out of the car and started to walk onto Teddy's yard to get me. As soon as she stepped foot on the yard, Teddy, who had been lying right by me, stood and advanced toward my mom with a low growl. My mom quickly backed up toward her car which satisfied Teddy who then came back and plopped down next to the trough. Irritated, my mom paced back and forth by the car a few times, puffing on a cigarette, before picking up a stick and attempting to walk back onto the yard again to get me. Teddy stood again, the hairs on his back bristling upward, bared his teeth and let out a more menacing growl. This convinced my mom not to step on that yard again. She tried yelling to me, "Philip, you get out of that water and get in my car!" I yelled back, "Ha ha, you can't get me," and continued to play in the water, convinced there was nothing she could do about the situation. "You're getting a spanking when you get home," she shouted to me before driving off.

I didn't care because at the moment I had Teddy as my protector. Eventually, of course, I had to go home, and true to her word, I got a spanking. Teddy was a good dog to me, and he just thought he was doing his job by watching over me and his home. My mom didn't think Teddy was such a good dog that day, but she still let me go down and play with him after that incident.

Hard Luck

It could have been bad choices, bad luck, or a combination of both, but people I grew up around seemed to have tragic things happen to them with astounding frequency. This was the case with Alphonse Gerken, an amiable guy I hung around with at times. He also was my teammate in school athletics, as well. Alphonse was a big guy who got along with people and never seemed mean like so many of those around us. But he was a bad luck magnet. In middle school we all had to pass a basic physical to participate in sports. Our school provided a doctor who came to the school to give them, but if you didn't pass, you had to see your family doctor for a more rigorous physical. This cost money, which most of us did not have. Part of the basic physical was to pee in a cup for testing. We were all handed a plastic cup with our name on it and told to go back into the toilet area, and then bring the cup back to the medical personnel for testing. Several guys couldn't produce a specimen.

Hard luck Alphonse told everyone he could pee a lot, so he provided the urine sample for seven other guys on our team. Well, there turned out to be something wrong with the urine and all those guys had to see their own doctors in order to participate. A couple of them were so poor they just didn't compete that season since they couldn't afford to pay for a new physical.

Alphonse's misfortune continued when he was in an argument with a guy who owed him money. The guy ended up grabbing a shotgun and shooting Alphonse. The blast grazed his face, taking out a portion of his forehead and one of his eyes. He became blind in that eye and wore a black pirate's patch to cover the damaged eye. Not long after that, Alphonse was on his motorcycle when a car hit him and he lost a leg at the hip. He faced a lot of tough situations for someone who was still a teenager.

He did get married a few years later, and he and his wife had a baby. One of my relatives also knew Alphonse and his wife, and one night she was babysitting their child. She got tired at about 10:00 PM so she took the baby to bed with her. When Alphonse and his wife came to get their baby at 2:00 AM, more bad luck had come their way. The baby was dead. It was devastating to everyone. It was ruled crib death, but it was another tragedy Alphonse had to face and then move on.

One spring, Alphonse was in a small boat fishing on the Big Sioux River when his boat capsized. The winter ice and snow had just melted and the river was not only cold but the current was turbulent and swift. Alphonse hung onto the boat which was being swept down river toward the perilous river spillway. If he were to be swept over the spillway, his chance of survival was next to none. His screaming caught the attention of people on shore who contacted the authorities. Just before Alphonse was swept over the spillway, the rescue crew got a net stretched across the river and plucked him from the frigid waters. Following this incident, the newspaper ran a story titled "Alphonse, A Man of Bad Luck." Alphonse moved away from Sioux Falls with his wife. I always admired Alphonse for having the intestinal fortitude to bounce back from all these tragedies while continuing to remain a good guy to be around.

A Mother's Scream

In Norton-Froehlich, crazy things were happening all the time. It seemed that there was never any peace. Have you ever heard a mother's scream? I call what I heard that day a mother's scream; it will bore into your soul and you will never forget it. I have bad dreams where I can hear that mother's shriek, but obviously in the area I grew up I was no stranger to hearing screams. Yet early one morning I was startled awake by the most horrible screaming I had ever heard. My first thought was "what the hell is that?" My second thought was to load a gun, yet in my panic-stricken hurry to get it loaded I kept fumbling the shells. Finally the shells slid into the gun's magazine. Then came a pounding on our door with the shrieking right outside. It was like something out of a bizarre horror film. My dad was not home, probably on a two or three day drunk, so my mom reluctantly opened the door. The young woman who lived just down from us ran into our place screaming that horrible sound. I noticed she was barefoot, and her three month old baby was in her arms. The baby was all discolored a dark bluish-grey. It just looked dead. The frantic woman began running in circles around our place, knocking things over. My mom grabbed the hysterical woman and wrestled the baby from her grip. My mom placed the baby on our table and tried to breathe into its mouth. "Oh no, no, no, oh please!" the mother wailed. Then my mom snatched up the baby and ran out to her car and jumped in and the hysterical woman jumped in with her. My mom sped away from our place heading toward the hospital. My sister said to me, "That baby is dead." We found out when my mom returned that the baby was indeed dead. A friend had just dropped the mother off from working an overnight shift and she found her baby in that condition. She had run to our place as she had no car or phone. Her live-in boyfriend had watched the baby that night. An investigation was done but turned out inconclusive, but people assumed it was probably Shaken Child Syndrome or suffocation. Just another crazy day in Norton-Froehlich.

I was exposed a second time to a mother's scream one day after school. The bus had just dropped me off on the tar road leading into

Norton-Froehlich. It was a nice spring day and I still recall the smell of lilac flowers in the air. I was walking along with a friend on the shoulder of the road as there were no sidewalks in our area. Walking alone about half a block ahead of us was Jimmy, a kid in my grade who I hung around with at times. A car came driving erratically down the road and I heard a muffled "thud." I looked up just in time to see Jimmy fly through the air like a rag doll. When Jimmy hit the road his head split open like an egg. We were the first ones to him and I could see he was dead. There was a huge pool of blood around his head and brain matter that looked greenish-grey hung eight inches out of the back of his head. I stared at Jimmy's unblinking eyes. His eyes had a faraway gaze. I then ran to get my mom while my friend went to call the sheriff and ambulance. When we got back to the accident site a small crowd of people had gathered. Apparently someone had run to get Jimmy's mother and from a block away I heard that horrible "mother's scream," the scream that bores into your mind forever. The scene was so gruesome I remember two men running and tackling Jimmy's mother and dragging her away from the site, yet that mother's scream went on and on. I did go to his funeral a few days later and it was a difficult service with loud sobbing everywhere. One thing that remains vivid in my memory is that horrible blood stain. Nobody took the initiative to hose it off the road. The first week it was a gooey mess that was covered with flies. After that it turned into a huge dark stain that was on that road all summer and fall only disappearing after the long winter. The crazy thing is, Jimmy's family had to go by that stain everyday as that road was the only access to their place. To this day I can go back to Norton-Froehlich and point out exactly where that blood stain was, and when I smell lilacs, I think of that day.

Donald (Becker) Moeller

Norton-Froehlich contained more than its share of violent and dangerous people. You learned not to trust anyone and to keep to yourself. I lived three units down from Donald Moeller who was executed in Sioux Falls in the fall of 2012 for the rape and murder of a young girl. I grew up knowing him as Donny Becker as he didn't know who his real father was and took on the last name of the guy his mom lived with at the time. Donny was the same age as my oldest sister, and he was dangerous even as a kid. He was always grimy and wore smelly clothes. He had dirt encrusted around his neck and caked under his fingernails. He had dark, hateful eyes void of emotion. Donny was someone you didn't turn your back on.

Before he was executed, the newspaper ran a lengthy story about our neighborhood and the horrible childhood he endured. I know for a fact that that story was correct because I lived the life and knew what he lived through, too. The story told how Donny, as a little child, had been tethered with a rope outside, tied up like a dog while the adults were drinking inside. The psychologist who worked with Donny in prison said that the most damaging thing to him was the open hatred and rejection Donny experienced from his mother. She made it clear that she hated him. She beat him mercilessly, and one time knocked him unconscious with a hot frying pan from the stove. She never used his name, preferring to call him 'bastard.' She constantly told him he was useless. She never wanted a son and would make him wear a dress when he was a small boy. His mother would walk around the house naked in front of Donny, and then she would wake him up late at night and make him watch her perform sexual acts with men she'd picked up in bars.

They celebrated no Christmas in their dark, joyless home, and Donny never had Christmas presents. The boys shared a bare mattress on the grimy floor with no sheets or pillows, and the mattress was blackened with years of dirt. So the little boy developed into the monster who lived a few houses down from me, the boy who finally met his demise with a lethal injection to the arm.

I recall one day when a friend and I were walking through a field and a bullet whizzed right by our heads. If you've ever been shot at, you never forget the sound. The bullet sounded like a giant bumble bee screeching *zzzzzzzzzzzng* and then a loud *crack* as it passed our heads. We turned and froze just in time to see Donny duck behind his house about fifty yards behind us.

Another time I overheard my oldest sister and Donny having a heated verbal exchange. There were no adults around, and I was standing just inside our front door with my sister while Donny was out on the street.

"F--- you, Donny, you dirty creep!" my sister yelled

"F--- you, you little whore!" he shot back.

"At least we're not a bastard like you. We know who our dad is."

The air changed in an instant. Donny tensed, then sprinted toward the door at full speed.

My sister quickly flipped the lock on our screen door and stepped back. Donny kicked the door in, busting most of the wood frame. I just stood there terrified as Donny grabbed my sister by the throat and slammed her against a wall.

"You little bitch!" he screamed. "If you ever say that again I'll kill you! I'll slit your throat!" To our relief, he turned and left.

Years later, when Donny raped and murdered that little girl, the autopsy listed the cause of death as a slit throat.

Smoe Hunt

Growing up, weekends were filled with uncertainty, arguments, and irritation. Many of our Friday and Saturday nights would be interrupted with the announcement by my mom to get in the car, an old Rambler with a smashed-in front end from an accident, to go find my dad. My sisters and I referred to this as a "Smoe Hunt." My dad's name was Joe, but we called him Smoe in reference to a little dive of a bar that he used to frequent called Smoe's Bar. It was a little cubicle of a bar located in a run-down area of town that bordered the stockyards and meat packing plant. The bar's logo was a picture of the 'Kilroy was here' man, which hung over the one grimy window in the front of the bar. Inside along the bar were 8 stools with metal legs and plastic seat covers, all of which bore either a cigarette burn, small tear, or a patch of duct tape. There were also three booths along the wall. At any time of day you'd find an assortment of lushes and winos puffing away on smokes while enjoying the dark dismal atmosphere and exchanging drunken points of view while Johnny Cash sang *Ring of Fire* in the background.

My dad was such a hard-core drunk that when he drank up the last of the booze at our house, he'd start drinking the Vick's Formula 44 cough medicine or Scope mouthwash. Sometimes he'd leave and go on two or three-day drunks and most likely spend the nights with other women. The Smoe hunt consisted of my mom driving us kids around and sending us into low-rent bars late at night to try to find him. I'd get into arguments with my sisters as to whose turn it was to go into a particularly rough establishment that none of us wanted to enter.

One night, as I reluctantly entered into the haze of yet another smoke-filled bar, a middle-aged lady with too much makeup grabbed me in a tight bear hug.

"Oh, look at the cute little boy," she slurred to her friend. The smell of stale cigarettes and fresh whiskey on her breath made me sick. The friend, wobbling in her chair with a silly grin on her face, was only saved from falling onto the floor by propping herself up on the table with one elbow, head in her hand. This happened all the time. Drunken women smelling of cheap perfume would grab and hug and sometimes kiss me, which just added to the already embarrassing task of looking for my drunken dad. In some bars there were strippers dancing on a back stage, and none of the bartenders ever told me to leave.

After a while the bartenders began to recognize me and would tell me right away, "Hey kid, your dad isn't in here."

It was humiliating. Most of the time we never found Smoe, but I do remember finding him at times and helping him stagger out to our car where we'd get him shoved into the backseat. If he got violent in the bar, we'd run back to the car, and my mom would speed away with him trying to chase after the car.

Bullies and the Bus from Hell

I was bussed to four different schools before high school, and my mom always said, "Well, I guess that principal doesn't want the Norton-Froehlich kids anymore, either."

And I can't say that I would blame principals as that bus carried a full load of trouble on board. Riding that bus was a lesson in self-defense every day. I feared stepping foot into this enormous vehicle packed with angry kids who were hungry to find their next victim. These were the days before anyone protected kids from bullies, and riding that bus exposed us to the worst bullying imaginable. I used to walk several blocks away from where the bus was to pick me up so I could get to the first pick-up spots in Norton-Froehlich. This allowed me to get a seat toward the front of the bus.

The back of the bus was where Donny (Becker) Moeller and the other older kids sat. The back was where the worst bullying occurred, so other kids learned to get to the front, too, but many times I was forced to the back of the bus. Whoever was unlucky enough to end up back there was kicked mercilessly for the entire trip, including many well-placed kicks to the privates. These older kids stabbed us with needles and pencils and took special delight in being able to smash a lunch if it was in a paper sack. I was fortunate enough to have my metal Rifleman lunch box.

Part of the fear was due to not knowing what they were going to do next. I never had my hair set on fire, but I saw them do it to other kids and always wondered what fresh hell they might invent the next day. Girls were grabbed and fondled, and none of us knew anything about sexual harassment back then. These older kids were as tough as grown men. Once, a bus driver did attempt to stop some particularly bad incident that I don't recall now years later, and one of these older kids punched him in the nose, causing it to bleed profusely. That kid was kicked off the bus, but the drivers learned to ignore all the commotion and focus on driving the bus.

The worst part was worrying that a group of bullies would get off at my bus stop to start a fight out of sight of any witnesses. This happened frequently. One day, a kid we called Maggot, who was two years older than me, kicked me in the privates when I was moving to find a seat on the bus. Maggot didn't like this nickname one bit, but his kick hurt so much that I blurted out, "F--- you, Maggot!" The Maggot had beady eyes that were set too close together, discolored teeth, and an odd body odor. I feared him as much as anyone, but on that day the name just slipped out.

"Oh, you think you're tough enough to call me Maggot, huh? I'll tell you what: I'm not getting off at my bus stop. I'm getting off at yours!" was his response.

"I'm not fighting you. I'm not fighting someone two years older and a lot bigger than me," I said.

"You don't have to fight, smart ass. I'm just going to pound you anyway."

So, I had to ride all the way to Norton-Froehlich sick to my stomach knowing what was coming. As he promised, Maggot did not get off at his stop, and neither did about a dozen other kids who rode to my drop off so they could see me take a butt-kicking. As soon as we all spilled out of the bus, kids pushing and rushing in eagerness to see a fight, I quickly attempted a smooth getaway. But Maggot followed, kicking me in the butt and back of my legs and telling me to turn around so he could give it to me in the face.

CRACK! A loud sound startled everyone and someone screamed. I quickly turned around to see that Maggot was on the ground. It just so happened that I was friends with, of all people, one of Donny's brothers. Let me tell you, Donny's brother was as violent and tough of a kid as you'd find in our neighborhood, and no one wanted to mess with him. He had come out of nowhere and blind-sided Maggot with a devastating punch. As Maggot lay on the ground, Donny's brother kicked him in the face and head until he was a bloody mess. Then he turned on the crowd of kids and said, "Oh, so you all like to see someone get an ass-kicking, huh? Well, if any of you are still here in ten seconds, you get what Maggot just got!"

Needless to say, the street was deserted in an instant. I walked back to my house with Donny's brother, and he told me he'd skipped school that day and was just walking down the street when he saw what the Maggot was doing to me. That's why he hadn't been on the bus that afternoon. Maggot was one bully who never bothered me again. But growing up being bullied turned me into a bully, too, and I said and did mean things to other kids, as well. I would hide in bushes with a BB gun and shoot at kids. One time two girls were walking down the street, and I took aim at the closest girl. I was an excellent shot and I hit her right in the butt, which is where I was aiming. She started jumping up and down yelling, "A hornet stung me." That made my day. It was so funny to me that I had to cover my mouth to hold in my laugh so I wouldn't be discovered hiding in the bushes that served as my sniper's nest.

I was mean to my friends, too, at times. I often hung out with a boy a year younger than me named Chris. We were all poor, but this kid was really poor coming from a family with seven kids. We were making designs with a junky Spirograph of mine. Pieces were broken and missing which caused the little plastic wheels to keep falling out of place.

"I'm gonna throw this away. It's junk," I complained, gathering up the pieces.

"Can I have it?" Chris asked eagerly.

I thought for just a moment.

"Yeah, if I can spit in your mouth three times." I don't know what inspired me to want to do that, but he agreed.

"You don't have to swallow them, but you have to hold the first two in your mouth while I work up the third one."

I can't believe he was that desperate for a broken toy, but he was. I told him to tip his head back and open his mouth. He looked like a baby bird in a nest with his mouth open. I spit the first one into his mouth. I then made him wait for a while for the second spit. Then I really made him wait for the third one. He spit it all out, gagging. When I gave him the Spirograph, he got really happy and ran home. Incidentally, that kid also grew to be 6' 4" and 260 lbs, was a star high school football player, and went on to play college football. I ran into Chris years later, and he was the pastor of a church.

In the late 60's, I was intrigued with all the current events I heard on the news about the Vietnam War. I paid close attention to information about booby traps, trip wire explosives, and other devices used by the enemy as well as our own special forces. I used this knowledge to create my own booby traps and used unsuspecting neighborhood kids to try them out.

One neighbor I hung around had four siblings younger than us. Their dad was a big, heavy guy who'd acquired the nickname Hubba Tubba Tony. These younger kids were all kind of chunky, too, so we called them the Hubba Tubba kids. The 2nd youngest looked just like Barney Rubble with his big nose and close-set eyes. I often set up various contraptions and booby traps for the Hubba Tubba kids just to be mean. I'd conceal a nail or sharp tacks under a piece of newspaper or in the grass and then lure a victim to the area. Kids always ran barefoot in the summer in Norton-Froehlich so my foot traps worked well. They'd scream and hop around when they stepped on one of my traps, and I'd say, "How did that get there?" I was sneaky about not being seen planting the device.

Once I ran a trip wire low in the grass that stretched from a fence to a tree, and I got a Hubba Tubba to run a race against me through this area. Letting the kid get ahead of me and thinking he was winning was all part of the plan, and I was delighted when he flew through the air after he hit the trip wire. He landed hard and I thought he'd broken an arm but it was only injured. I got caught a couple times booby-trapping the Hubba Tubbas, and again my mom told me I was going to end up in prison.

Another trap involved filling a Hamms beer can full of water and balancing it on the top of a door with the door slightly open-maybe two inches. When a victim pushed the door open and stepped through, the can would drop and hit them on the head. Of course they knew I had set some traps, but I was good at rotating my traps so the locations and time between traps varied which increased the odds of my success.

In junior high we would experiment with food tampering at lunch just to be mean. We'd distract a kid and drop ½ an Alka Seltzer in his milk, or we'd put a big pinch of habanero powder into a kid's food. In the showers for P.E., we'd offer kids a shampoo bottle that was spiked with Nair hair remover hoping they'd go bald. It didn't work, of course. I did so many harsh things to other kids, but when you're treated meanly, you start to fight, and you start to become a bully.

We had fun with a few food dares, too. A kid named Piff always ate at our table. I don't know how he got his nickname, but Piff had kind of a deformed arm. One arm was bent and smaller than the other arm. Piff told us he'd broken it when he was little and his mom never took him in for a cast. Piff loved the chocolate pudding cups we sometimes got for lunch. These cups were served about half full. Piff always begged for everyone else's chocolate pudding, and one day he said, "I could eat 50 of these puddings!" I said, "Bullshit, Piffer. No way could you eat 50." He then made me a $5 bet that he could. So the next time we had chocolate pudding, two other kids went around the lunch room with me and collected 50 of them. I lost the bet, too. Piff sat there and he ate every one of those desserts. None of us could believe it. We continued eating our lunch, and a few minutes later Piff turned to me and said, "I don't feel too good. My stomach feels sugary." There was a short pause, and then Piff projectile vomited a huge black spray into the air that hit the table and everyone nearby as well as the wall and floor. Piff won the bet, but he also got sugar poisoning.

Building Bombs and Lessons from Big Jim

Fffffsssstttt! "Oh, no! We must not have sealed it tight enough. It was a dud. Does your dad have any more black powder for his muzzle loading gun?"

"No, we can't take any more black powder or he'll notice it's missing."

So we went back to cutting open hundreds of firecrackers and bottle rockets to get the gun powder we needed. Besides booby traps for the Hubba Tubbas, my friend Little Jim and I experimented with building "bombs." Little Jim, who was from my neighborhood, was my bomb-building partner. He was called Little Jim because everyone aptly called his dad Big Jim; he was a burly, strapping man with a gravelly voice and a big, bushy beard. Little Jim and I would spend all day building a bomb. We tested the results of different sizes and types of canisters filled with the fine particles obtained from Big Jim's hunting supplies for our homemade bombs. We filled small cans, glass bottles, and plastic tubes with explosives and some provided huge blasts. We would detonate our bombs down by the Big Sioux River, which wasn't far from our house. We probably would have been charged with something if we'd ever been caught discharging bombs, but our antics remained undiscovered.

After removing all the fuses from the firecrackers, we connected them together for one long fuse. We used duct tape and dripped candle wax to seal the openings of the bomb canisters. We always got Little Jim's brother, Wendell, to light our bombs while we hid behind a tree for protection from the explosion. On bare feet, in his knee-length fringe shorts and no shirt, his freckled face taut, Wendell lit the fuse and began sprinting for cover when, *kaboom!* The device went off before he'd reached safety. Wendell fell to the ground with a shout, and when we ran to his aid, we discovered shrapnel lodged in the back of his legs, arms, and neck. He had to go to the hospital to have the shrapnel removed and to get a tetanus shot. The hospital did not call the police about this injury; they let the dad deal with it. Big Jim whipped Little Jim with a razor strap, which is an actual leather strap used by barbers to sharpen a straight razor. When my mom found out, she just yelled, "You're going to end up in prison some day!" That ended our bomb-building days.

Big Jim lived like a mountain man and would trap food for his family. He was raising the boys alone since his wife had left him. A typical supper consisted of cooked rabbits or possum he'd caught in one of his traps. He was also a poacher and would shoot animals out of season, as well. One day, Big Jim took Little Jim and me to hunt pheasants on an Indian Reservation in South Dakota since he had a buddy who was Native American. Many adults from my neighborhood were not proper role models for young people, and Big Jim proved to be no exception on this particular hunt. Not only were we hunting without a state or tribal license, but Big Jim was a meat hunter and had us shoot as much game as we could kill. In two days, we shot almost 60 pheasants- enough to put someone in jail.

Big Jim would send us up to a ranch house to get permission to hunt near the resident's home. At one house, we knocked on the door but nobody was there. The people must have been stocking up on food supplies for the long winter because there were at least 75 sacks of groceries sitting all over in the entry way and kitchen. We went back to the car and told Big Jim that nobody was around and then mentioned the unusual amount of groceries we'd seen.

"Why the hell didn't you two grab some of those food sacks? What were you thinking?" He yelled and then scowled and shook his head as if we'd done something wrong for not stealing the groceries. Little Jim and I slunk back and took two sacks each. While driving away, Big Jim told us to look in the bags to see if there was "a loaf of bread and a ring of red," which was ring bologna.

That night, we slept at his Native American friend's shack on the reservation. We came from a poor neighborhood, but it was nothing compared to the reservation. What we saw was almost indescribable. The shack we stayed in looked like something that even a goat would refuse to live in. There were burlap feed bags or boards tacked over every opening and not a single pane of glass left in any window. Overgrown weeds and tall prairie grass surrounded the shack, covering any trace of a path or driveway. One end of the rickety porch rested on the ground while the other end was propped up with a small stack of wooden boards. Not a trace of paint remained anywhere. There was no place for us to sleep in the one-room structure. Not all reservations resemble this, but the conditions in some areas of this reservation were deplorable. Big Jim and his buddy were already drunk, and I wanted to sleep. We couldn't lie down in Big Jim's car because there were holes in the seats and springs stuck out all over. We asked where we could sleep, and the Indian said, "Sleep out on the porch. There are some carpets and rugs you can cover up with." So, we went out and tried to sleep on the front porch using a damp, musty carpet and a few dirty rugs for warmth. Not only did we toss and turn all night, but dirt and grit kept falling out of rugs and into my hair, mouth, and ears.

We hunted the next day, and the same scenario occurred the next night. After both of the adults passed out, I told Little Jim, "Let's put your dad in the back seat and go back to Sioux Falls." So we got Big Jim to his feet and half-carried him to the car where we managed to get him in the backseat. Little Jim drove all the way back home even though he didn't have a driver's license since we were both only 14 years old.

Little Jim's family moved to Redfield, South Dakota when Big Jim got hired to work at the Redfield State Institute. This was a place that housed people who were wards of the state due to being mentally disabled or legally insane. Life was better for Little Jim and Wendell since their dad finally had a good income working as an orderly helping to care for the residents. They all moved back to our neighborhood about a year later after Big Jim got fired. He probably broke a lot of rules as he was often reprimanded for upsetting the residents, but there were two incidents in particular that are memorable. The people in this institution were primarily adults but many had the mental capacity of small children. They were very excited when Christmas was approaching because they looked forward to Santa coming. Big Jim told them that Santa Claus died of a heart attack, so he wouldn't be coming anymore. It upset the residents so much that a letter of discipline was put in his file. But then Easter came and Big Jim told them not to expect any Easter eggs or candy because he had shot and killed the Easter Bunny during hunting season.

With the lessons we learned from role models like Big Jim, it's not surprising that we built bombs and got in all kinds of trouble.

The Skull and Big Toe Incidents

After Big Jim got fired from the Redfield State Institute, he got a job running an earth moving machine to expand the interstate highway system in western South Dakota. One day, I went over to see Little Jim, and there was a human skull on their table. I asked Little Jim what the skull was from. He said, "My dad found it when he was working." The skull was in their house for about a week when some men from the state came and took it away and fired Big Jim. It turned out that Big Jim had unearthed several human bones but didn't tell anyone. The foreman happened to see the bones and questioned Big Jim about it. Big Jim readily admitted taking the human skull, not seeing how that would be a problem in any way. It turns out that it had come from an old Native American burial ground, and due to this the bones were properly reinterred and the interstate was diverted around that sacred area. Big Jim should not have taken that skull, and he deserved to lose his job again.

A crazy coincidence is that I had another friend named Jim who also had a little brother named Wendell. That same summer, Jim was giving his brother Wendell a ride on the handlebars of his bicycle. Wendell had on shorts and was barefoot. As they rode down the road, the bicycle hit a bump and Wendell's foot swung into the front tire spokes. The rotating tire spokes sliced Wendell's big toe clean off. Screaming in pain and bleeding profusely, Jim quickly rode Wendell back to their house. Their dad drove Wendell to the hospital. About half an hour later, the dad called the house and said, "Get a glass full of ice, and go get that big toe. I'm coming home to get it so they can sew it back on." Jim got the ice and ran to where the accident had occurred. He found all the blood in the street, but the big toe was nowhere in sight. Hattie, an old lady who lived in the neighborhood, was out in her yard. Jim yelled to her, "Have you seen that toe that was cut off of Wendell's foot?" Hattie replied, "No, but Bubba was eating something out there in the street." Bubba was a big, brown hunting dog from the neighborhood. So, Bubba got a snack, and Wendell lost a big toe.

Every time we saw Bubba, we'd yell, "Get home, toe-eater!" We also found out that you really do need a big toe in order to balance on one leg. We would have Wendell show people how he could balance on the leg with all five toes on the foot. If he tried to balance on the foot without the big toe, he'd tip right over. We knew then why people always told us to wear shoes when riding a bicycle.

Animal House

I learned the secrets to perfecting a scam at a very young age. The lessons started right at home. My dad was a yardman at the stockyards where his job was to place livestock into holding pens before they were auctioned or went to slaughter. Many nights after a pig or sheep gave birth in a holding pen, my dad would steal the newborn animal and bring it home.

Using two old doors propped on their sides, my dad would build a pen in a corner of our house. He'd put newspaper on the floor of the pen, and we'd raise the animal right in our home. At times the house stunk like a rank barn. My dad would run an extension cord and rig up a heat light to shine on the newborn animal. We'd bottle feed the baby until it was ready for solid food. Then my dad would steal grain from the stockyards to feed it. When the animal got to a certain age, my dad would take it back to the stockyards and put it into the auction sale and make some money from the scam. There were times he didn't sell the animal and instead raised it to feed size. Once the animal was fattened up, he'd take it out back, shoot it, and tie it upside down to a pole so he could skin and gut it. This was the most upsetting because then we had to eat an animal we'd bottle fed and had come to view as a pet.

Yuck

We never went completely without food, but sometimes we scraped the bottom of the barrel. My dad blew a lot of money on booze, gambling, and other women. He liked to come across as the big shot and would buy other drunks round after round of alcohol. We called these people his 'boozin' buddies.' He would also drive down to Sioux City and spend money on greyhound dog races. He knew where to find back alley gambling games that took place out of view of the law. He frequented an illegal card room in the back of a billiards hall where he'd play poker for hours on end. During the summer, when my mom was at work, he'd take me with him, and I'd have to sit in the dark card room for what seemed like an eternity. It smelled of a combination of cigar and cigarette smoke, chewing tobacco, and onions from the sandwiches they'd order from the lunch counter in the billiards room. It made me nauseous, and I just wanted to go outside and play. The room was mostly bare except for the table in the middle and spittoons by the wall near where the men sat. I was amazed at the accuracy and distance with which they could spit the slimy brown tobacco juice.

When my dad gambled all our money away, we often ate mustard sandwiches for dinner and put water on our breakfast cereal because there was no milk. My dad came up with ways to put food on the table without having to skimp on his drinking and gambling. He'd shoot pigeons out of the wood rafters at the stockyards with a .22 rifle and bring them home in a box. We had to skin the breasts out and fry them up. I hated the taste of pigeon. He'd bring me to work with him at night at times and let me sit in the stockyards with the .22 rifle and shoot rats. These huge rats snuck along the livestock pens, and I became an excellent shot at a young age taking them out one at a time. We lucked out and never ended up having to eat the rats!

We also raised tame rabbits for food. Our rabbits had many babies which we raised to a certain size. Then my dad would butcher them for food. I loved animals and viewed all the rabbits as pets so I always got sick on nights we had floured and fried rabbit for supper because I didn't know if I was eating Pinky or Black Ears.

In the fall, after the turtles had dug into the mud to hibernate, we'd go turtling for food. My dad brought us to various duck ponds where we'd wade in the water probing the mud with long steel rods that were bent into a hook on one end. We'd probe until the rod hit something solid that made a *thud* that vibrated up through the rod. That meant it was a snapper's shell. Now, using the hooked end of the probe, we pulled the turtle out of the mud. We carried burlap gunny sacks so we'd have a place to put the turtles. I was always afraid I'd get bit by a big snapper, yet I never did. When we butchered the turtles, the snappers' mouths would keep biting and even latch onto sticks after their heads were cut off. We fried and ate the turtle meat, and I must admit they were tasty. One time I found a snapping turtle that weighed over fifty pounds. A conservation officer estimated it to be about 100 years old. I got my picture in the newspaper holding the turtle with the hooked rod. He made for a tough and chewy dinner that week.

The day I hated the most was chicken day. My dad would bring home two huge gunny sacks of live chickens to butcher. He'd bring out a chopping block and whack the chickens' heads off, one after another. Chickens would run around the yard, leap into the air, and spurt blood all over even after their heads were chopped off. At times, four or five headless chickens would be running around at the same time. It seemed that no matter where I was or where I ran that these headless chickens would run right at me. My dad laughed at my fear and always made me go around and pick up the chickens that finally dropped to the ground. Right when I'd pick one up it would start to flutter and flap all over again. I hated the whole day. When it was over, it looked like a devil's butcher shop.

Once the chickens were gathered my dad would boil water in a huge copper pot. He added wax to the water and we dipped the headless chickens in there to make them easier to pluck. Plucking took all day to complete. The smell of the wet feathers with wax on them made me sick. Many years passed before I could eat chicken again.

Early Goals

Franklin Elementary School was one of those turn-of-the-century schools constructed from large blocks of purplish granite found in the rock quarry. The doors and woodwork had turned dark brown from age; its windows were tall and wide allowing for natural light to stream through. This was the third elementary school I attended, and it was in this building where I met a special teacher who helped shape my life.

Judy Jasper was the P.E. teacher at Franklin who believed in discipline. She commanded respect and had a no-nonsense attitude. There was no goofing around and no time wasted. Her class operated like a well-oiled machine. She was the first person to teach me to reach goals by working so hard that it seemed I was pushing beyond my limits. This was during the Vietnam War, and her P.E. classes took on a military atmosphere.

"Open ranks!" She'd call out, and we'd wordlessly move in double time to preassigned spots on the gymnasium floor.

"Closed ranks!" And we all moved forward to the front line placing our toes precisely on the red line and standing tall with our hands folded behind our backs.

Running obstacle courses and climbing the rope to the ceiling were common class activities. While many of my classmates dreaded the intensity of P.E. and feared our teacher, I loved it and thrived in this environment with consistent rules and structure. Boys did pull-ups and girls did the bar hang at the start and end of every class. Upper body strength was a weakness for most students, and Miss Jasper aimed to eliminate this weakness in all of us. All year long she yelled encouragement to me while I was on the pull-up bar.

"Philip, don't stop. Get two more pull-ups. Don't give up."

My muscles ached, I strained, and I worked hard to do what she said.

On the wall in our gym was a huge record board with all the President's Physical Fitness Test records and the names of the students who held the individual records.

Miss Jasper would say, "Philip, you can get your name on that record board."

Years later I asked Miss Jasper why she called me Philip when everyone else called me Phil. She told me she liked the name Philip.

The President's Physical Fitness Test was given each spring and was a big deal in our school as Franklin Elementary was the record holder in the state of South Dakota for having the most students achieve this award. That state record would go on for over twenty years during Miss Jasper's reign at the school. I saw on our record board that the pull-up record for my grade was twenty-one. I began to visualize my name on that board every time Miss Jasper told me I could do it. I continued to work hard in her class.

That spring, with my whole class watching on, I did twenty-nine pull-ups, breaking the 5th grade record by several pull-ups. The day I saw my name on that record board I swelled with pride. I did it! The next spring I did thirty-two pull-ups to set a new 6th grade school record. Beaming, I sat down with my class to watch the next person take their turn at the bar. My new record lasted all of ten minutes when my best friend, Mike Hadrath, took his turn and did forty-four pull-ups. Amazing. Mike had taken second place to me the year before when he did twenty-eight pull-ups-one shy of what I did. Mike's individual record was on that board for twenty years. Miss Jasper finally decided to retire his record since students were no longer attempting to beat this unbelievable pull-up record.

Over the years, Mike and I had spent a lot of time together. We were the starting point guards on our basketball teams, we played baseball together, went trick-or-treating together, and hung out every chance we had. When Mike was murdered a few years later, I mourned his death for a long time.

Bloody Halls

Axtell Junior High took in students from Norton-Froehlich as well as from the North side, West Soo, and the overflow students from the Indian boarding school. I don't know the history behind it, but most Native American kids in this school who were Crow hated the Native kids who were from one of the Sioux tribes. The fist fights between kids from these two Indian groups were frequent and bloody.

One Native American student at our school, Wally, was a brutal fighter. At a house party one night, Wally beat a twenty-five year old man into unconsciousness. It was the first time I realized that a fifteen-year-old kid could be tougher than an adult man. Word spread all over town that Wally was a person to be feared. He was just one of the many tough kids who walked the halls at my school, and looking up to these kids as role models I embraced a new philosophy to live by during confrontations. I realized that there was a difference between a bully and a tough guy. Wally would have never thought to pick on someone weaker or smaller or disabled. But he was a guy you didn't mess with. I respected that.

Because of all the mean kids, I rarely went into a restroom out of fear of being jumped. One time a kid from Norton-Froehlich had a beef with me because I'd beaten up his brother who was in my grade. He was older but it seemed that in my neighborhood if you got in a fight with one family member, you had the whole clan to deal with. Out of necessity I was in the school restroom standing at the urinal when that kid rushed in behind me and out of nowhere punched me in the jaw so hard my head slammed into the tile wall. Trying to remain standing on unsteady feet, all I could see were stars just like in the cartoons when a character gets whacked on the head. I was knocked kind of goofy, and my mind was thinking in slow motion *whaaat's haappenning tooooo meeee?* With sparklies circling my head, I staggered to my left and as I bent forward at the waist he kicked me hard in the face. Then, that was it. It was all over. The kid got me back for beating up his little brother and walked out.

There were many times I came across fresh pools of blood or blood splatters in the hallway before the custodians arrived to clean it up. Later on, we'd all get the word as to who had been in the fight.

In order to maintain discipline, the teachers were hard-nosed and strict. In the early 1970's corporal punishment was still allowed, and no one would have ever dreamed of filing a law suit against a school or teacher. I saw students get hit, paddled, and slammed against walls. I was choked a couple of times by teachers and coaches. One science teacher was especially feared. He was 6' 3," 270 lbs, and mean. He was my science teacher, and was actually a very good and interesting teacher. One day in class we could hear a kid in the hallway yell, "F---you," to someone as he was walking past. The science teacher's head snapped up. He closed his book on the desk and stormed into the hall. We could hear slapping –*smack, smack*—a desperate choking sound, and someone getting slammed over and over into a metal locker. There were some muffled screams, and then our teacher appeared again in the doorway, his face beet red and he was breathing heavily. No one said a word. We all continued what we'd been doing as if none of us had noticed anything out of the ordinary.

This same teacher worked lunchroom duty, and he was just as strict there. He stood guard by where we dumped our trash and returned our trays. At the beginning of the year, and at regular intervals after that, he had announced to everyone that any food taken from the line was to be eaten. He did not believe in food being wasted. Being kids, we would often forget to tell the lunch servers not to give us things like corn or peas, so if food ended up on our tray, we had to eat everything or hope someone at our lunch table would eat it for us. A couple of times this teacher made me stay and finish all of my food. Once, two kids couldn't finish all their food so they had to go and sit in his science room until all the food was gone. One kid took three hours to finish. Eventually, some kids tried to be sneaky and smash any food they had left over into their milk carton. The science teacher got wise to this, and he would pick up a crunched milk carton before it was thrown in the trash. If it felt heavy, he'd open it up and make the offender eat the entire carton of mushed up gunk.

Two brothers ate at my lunch table every day. They were in the same grade because the older one had been held back two times in grade school. These brothers were poor and got free lunch tickets. These tickets had just enough punches to last for one month and then a new one would be issued. Quite often these brothers would be out of lunch punches as they had eaten double lunches earlier in the month. They always asked for everyone's leftovers so they were good kids to have at our table in case we had food we didn't want to eat and couldn't throw away. One day when they were out of punches, the younger brother stole a lunch. When the lunch lady turned away, he discreetly stepped out of line and came to our table. "Give me half of that!" the older brother demanded." "Hell no, I took the risk," replied the younger brother. The older one reached over to take some food, and his brother stuck a metal fork right in the top of his hand. It turned into a fist fight right in the cafeteria. The brothers got hauled to the principal's office and got three whacks each on their rear ends with the canoe paddle (which was a standard form of corporal punishment in our school.) All this because they were hungry.

I also saw my P.E. teacher knock a kid out in class one day. We were all sitting along the wall in a line with our backs to the wall. The P.E. teacher was holding a basketball and giving us instructions. Two kids were messing around and talking to each other. Suddenly, the teacher threw the basketball at them like a baseball pitch. The basketball hit one kid in the face and drove the back of his head into the cement wall. I looked over, and he was out cold. The kid just laid there until the school nurse came down and put an ice pack on his head when he woke up.

Many of the kids at my school were deviants and would do sick things. If they did not like you, a lock was essential for your locker. If you didn't have a lock they would pee all over your books and your jacket. Junior high was a rough time for me, but as with all things in my life, I learned to deal with it as it was nothing compared to my home life.

Gitchie Manitou Murders

On a cool Saturday evening in November of 1973, five carefree teenagers drove to Gitchie Manitou Park about fifteen miles east of Sioux Falls to camp overnight. They built a campfire and cooked food. The sunset lifted from the sky, dusk began to fall, and darkness filled the surrounding tree line until it faded into night. They added more wood to the fire, sang songs, laughed, and talked. People camped there frequently, and no one anticipated anything but a fun weekend.

Beyond the light of the campfire, three men watched and waited, biding their time until the right moment presented itself.

The teenagers were in the middle of telling stories when a shotgun blast pierced the night and one fell dead by the campfire. The terrified teens jumped to their feet as two more shots rang out, wounding two more of them. The last two campers ran off into the woods and attempted to hide.

The following morning, just as the sun was coming up, a man going to work saw something strange lying near the road at Gitchie Manitou. He got out of his vehicle and cautiously approached what had caught his attention. To his horror, he'd found the bodies of four teenage boys. The bodies were stiff with rigor mortis and the arms and legs were contorted in grotesque angles. Shotgun blasts had torn their bodies apart.

Monday morning while getting ready for school, I heard on the radio that my former best friend, Mike Hadrath, had been murdered. I became physically sick and threw up. Another one of the campers, Roger Essem, lived one block away from me. Stewart and Dana Baade were brothers who were acquaintances of mine. I got word that Roger's girlfriend had been kidnapped by the murderers and released near her home.

At the funeral home, it was obvious that Mike had been shot in the face with the shotgun. His face had been reconstructed, but I thought he looked horrible. I wished it had been a closed casket, but later on I found out that his mom and dad wanted the reconstruction done. They didn't want their last memory of Mike to be the way he looked when they identified his body at the morgue.

The killers were caught a week later after a massive manhunt. I didn't know many details of the murder and didn't see Roger's girlfriend for several years after that. When I ran into her at a shopping mall one night we talked briefly, and she was happy and talkative. I hoped she was doing as well as she appeared. To this day, I consider her an extraordinary person with strength and courage to have survived this ordeal.

Later on, I read the court records and other information on the details of that horrible night. When the first shot rang out, it was Roger, who fell down dead. The next two shots wounded Stewart and Dana as they'd started to run away. Mike ran and hid in a thicket.

While he was hiding, the killers yelled, "We're with the sheriff's department. Come out with your hands up where we can see them."

Mike reluctantly came out of hiding. The killers immediately shot Mike in the arm, and he fell to the ground and tried to play dead. This ploy didn't fool the killers who kicked him and told him to get up. They tied up Roger's girlfriend and rounded up the three wounded boys who they coldly finished off with several shotgun blasts. For some reason they did not kill the girl. Instead, one of the killers drove her back near her home and released her threatening that she'd better not tell any details. Obviously, she gave the authorities vital information that led to the murderers being apprehended: Allen, David, and James Fryer were a motley group of antisocial brothers who liked to stalk people around Gitchie Manitou at night. The three are currently serving life sentences as the state did not have the death penalty at the time.

Today, kids in the area say that Gitchie Manitou is haunted. Teenagers go there at night to party and frighten each other with scary stories. It's an especially popular place on Halloween. Gitchie Manitou does haunt one thing for sure; it haunts my mind.

Lucky to Be Alive

It was a mild winter day and a light blanket of snow covered the ground. It was the kind of day that would be perfect for sledding, skiing, or hunting. *Brrriiinngg.* I answered the phone, and it was my buddy Chuck Kruger.

"Phil, grab your .22 and come over to my place. We'll go rabbit hunting."

That sounded fun. Chuck and I often hunted pheasant, rabbit, or squirrel when the weather was good. I told him I'd be over shortly and loaded the hunting gear into my beat-up robin egg blue '67 Ford pick-up. With a hunting hat, bullets, gun case, and sack lunch in hand I was off.

I walked into Chuck's place ready to go, but he told me to relax awhile as he hadn't had time to eat yet. There sitting on Chuck's couch was a 7-year-old neighbor boy who lived nearby. Chuck dated his older sister, and this boy often came over to Chuck's place to watch television. He was one of the few people who had cable TV at the time so this kid loved coming over and watching cartoon channels. With the TV blaring in the background I settled into a chair and began to read the newspaper.

BANG!

A loud explosion echoed through the room, and my head snapped up to see the boy standing in the doorway holding Chuck's rifle. I smelled gunpowder. My ears were ringing. I jumped up and saw the boy's eyes were wide with terror. Before I could speak, he dropped the gun and raced out of the house. Running into the kitchen, I found Chuck staggering across the room before dropping to the floor. Panicking, I rushed to his side and knelt down.

"Chuck, where were you hit?" I yelled.

He let out a small moan as a reply.

I looked him over, lifting his shirt and turning him this way and that before finding a small spot of blood on the front of his blue jeans. The blood was right on the belt line of his jeans about four inches from the snap and zipper. I unsnapped his jeans, and saw a small puncture wound in his lower abdomen. It looked almost as if someone had jabbed him with a pencil. I rolled him to his side to check for an exit wound and reeled back in shock. The bullet had exited through his left butt cheek. The expression 'a bullet enters small but exits with devastation' held true; there was a hole the size of a baseball with fat and tissue hanging out in bloody shreds.

Too alarmed to think as clearly as I should have, I decided to drag Chuck to my pick-up and rush him to the hospital figuring it was faster than waiting for an ambulance to come all the way out to the housing area. Using all my strength I hauled him into the vehicle. He had one arm slung around my neck and was conscious enough now to stand on his own assisting me in getting him into the vehicle. I drove 75 mph most of the way to the emergency room completely distracted by his loud moaning the entire way there.

Chuck went into surgery and was very fortunate. The bullet just missed his bladder and femoral artery. When he was released from the hospital we dug that bullet out of the kitchen cabinet where it had lodged after passing through his body. He was left with a huge scar on his butt cheek.

A strange twist to that story is that Chuck worked in a lumber mill, and his job was to split logs by sending them through a machine with a huge circular saw. He had to wear a face and upper body shield because logs would explode from time to time if the machine hit a knot and would send high powered splinters everywhere. One morning, Chuck had turned around and bent over to pick up a log when the log behind him exploded into splinters. A large splinter the length of an arrow shot into his right butt cheek emerging out at an angle through his upper thigh.

He didn't have ambulance service on his insurance, and none of his co-workers would take him to the hospital because it was Saturday, and they were getting overtime so he had to drive himself to the emergency room. Chuck's car had a stick shift with a clutch. The splinter protruding out would not allow him to sit normally in the seat. He had to drive almost on his side in order to work the clutch and stick shift. He was rushed in for surgery at the hospital where he ultimately ended up with two badly scarred butt cheeks.

Fifteen years later I was in a billiards hall when a young man in his early twenties approached me.

"Hi, do you remember me?" he asked.

I told him I didn't. He didn't look familiar at all.

"I shot your friend," he said softly.

He told tell me how he had experienced bad dreams for a long time after shooting Chuck. He'd had to talk to a school counselor to help him deal with what he'd done. This serves as a great reminder about making sure loaded guns are never accessible to children.

More Gore

"Phew! What's the nasty smell?" my friend asked as we walked down a tar road in Norton-Froehlich on a warm summer day.

I could smell it, too. It was a sickly-sweet smell that hung heavy in the air. We fanned our hands in front of our faces and kept walking until the smell finally dissipated.

A few days later we found out that someone had committed suicide in a home near the foul-smelling road. The body wasn't discovered for more than a week. Apparently, a man's wife left him and took the children with her. In his despair, he'd put a shotgun in his mouth and blew the top of his head off.

Being curious, I went to the house with a friend so we could look through the windows. There were no curtains on the windows, and we could easily see inside. A huge blood splatter covered the center of the ceiling with little spots spread around covering the rest of the ceiling. Pieces of dried skin and brain were still visible, sticking out of the blood smears. We could also see the hole where the shot gun pellets had blown through the ceiling. It was a horrible sight. I always wondered how it ever got cleaned up because someone moved into the house a few months later. The strange thing is, the house is less than thirty yards from the blood stain left on the road after my friend Jimmy was hit by the automobile.

Patrick Pickering was another dangerous individual who lived close to me. He even looked rough. He had scars on his body, leathery skin, and was missing a front tooth. Patrick was in his twenties yet was dating a teenage girl, Lila Mae Scott, from our neighborhood. My mom warned me to stay clear of Patrick because he was involved in illegal activities and had a quick, hostile temper. Lila Mae was a few years older than me, and I thought she was very pretty. She had long, dark hair and green eyes.

A short distance from Norton-Froehlich, a pump house sits next to the bank of the Big Sioux River. The water runs slowly and smoothly in this area, and it is a dark greenish-brown color. Sycamores line the bank with branches that hang low over the water's edge. It was to this place where Patrick drove Lila Mae one evening with anger coursing through his veins.

When Lila Mae did not return home, her family posted missing person flyers around town. A couple of days later her body was discovered in the Big Sioux River. It didn't take the authorities long to solve the murder, and of course, it was Patrick Pickering.

It turns out that he'd been angry with Lila Mae and drove her to the pump house station. There he beat her to death with a tire iron from the trunk of his car. South Dakota hadn't voted for the death penalty at the time, so Pickering got a life sentence. In prison he murdered a fellow inmate a few years later by putting rat poison in the man's food. It was said that the poison was most likely provided to him by a corrupt guard or smuggled into the penitentiary during a visit. Patrick became so violent in prison that even long stretches of solitary confinement didn't change his behavior.

On the day I found out where Patrick had murdered Lila Mae, I went to the pump house with a friend. People are just drawn to seeing macabre things like murder sites. On the cement by the pump house were huge dried pools of blood with large clumps of her long hair pasted into it. The stench of death lifted off the hot cement as the blood and hair cooked in the afternoon heat. It was an eerie sight. I heard a neighbor tell my mom that Pickering had beaten Lila Mae's face so violently that she was unrecognizable. The family identified her by the rings she wore.

I was depressed after the murder. I agonized over the thought of this pretty young woman who was now a corpse after suffering at the hands of another Norton-Froehlich psychopath.

The only tar road leading into Norton-Froelich. It was on this road that my friend Jimmy was killed. Notice the absence of sidewalks.

Mike Hadrath (right) and I getting ready to leave for a basketball game. This photo was taken in 1970. Mike was murdered in 1973.

The pump house where Patrick Pickering murdered Lila Mae Scott.
There was always a lot of violence in my neighborhood.

PART TWO

MY STRUGGLE

In the beginning, there was wrestling.*

*See Genesis 32:22-30

One Foot on the Right Path

Brutality and bizarre behavior were the norm in people I grew up with, even with many kids I encountered at school. Yet aside from the rough environment in some of my schools, there was also a sense of structure and discipline that fulfilled a craving. With certain teachers, coaches, and programs I began to find areas in which I could excel. I began to develop a sense of confidence, pride, and self-worth.

In my 4th through 9th grade years I was the point guard on our basketball teams averaging over ten points a game. My good friend, Mike Hadrath, was the other point guard on our teams which was one reason I took it so hard when he was murdered at Gitchie Manitou with the other teenagers from my neighborhood. In two seasons of basketball I was the top free throw percent scorer in the city. When I was in 9th grade, my junior high school posted a flyer stating that there would be a split season so basketball players could try wrestling. I had no desire to wrestle and told my basketball coach my feelings on the subject.

"You'll try it like everyone else," was his clipped response.

That night I went down to my first wrestling practice expecting to see a boxing ring encased with ropes on all sides just like the ones I'd seen professional wrestlers use on television. I'd never even seen a wrestling mat. That season in wrestling I went undefeated in duals and went on to win the city, district, and regional tournaments. I did all this wearing tennis shoes and a P.E. t-shirt and shorts unlike my competitors who wore wrestling singlets and nice light-weight wrestling shoes. I beat many opponents who had wrestling backgrounds. At the AAU state meet I lost only one match. Maybe being trapped in a phone booth and forced to fight as a child actually turned out to benefit me in the long run.

The word of my wrestling accomplishments reached the head coach at Sioux Falls Washington High School. At the time, Washington housed about 2,600 students in a castle-like fortress with four levels built in 1908. It has always been a school where sports are held in high regard. Washington holds the distinction of winning more state football championships than any high school of any class in the United States.

Ray Wellman, the wrestling coach, was a balding but stocky and still muscular man who rarely smiled or showed any emotion unless it was in the heat of his team being on the verge of a win. When he patted someone on the back, they knew they'd earned it. When he came to my junior high and invited me to come up to the high school spring wrestling practices, I had no idea that a very special person had just entered my life. I was the only junior high wrestler invited to attend these practices. In practices that spring, I easily beat the high school kid in my weight division who'd been slated to be the varsity wrestler at Washington the next fall. I never played another basketball game.

Many eyes around the state were on the Washington varsity wrestling team to see if they'd be able to repeat a state championship as they had recently won the state title. As the only underclassman on that team I was expected to step up and perform at a very high level. There was always someone waiting to take my spot.

At the same time a change was beginning to take root in my life. For once, I had one foot on the right path. Being the lightest wrestler on the team I was always the first to go out and wrestle.

Before each meet, Coach Wellman would gather the varsity together, point at me, and say, "Momentum starts with you. You get the team on the plus side right away. Step it up and wrestle."

At times the pressure was enormous, but I thrived on being challenged. Several times in a dual Coach Wellman would move me up to a higher weight division after we had all weighed in. This was a coaching strategy to help Washington beat the opposing school. He thought I might get the win where our regular guy in that weight division might not. This was a strategy I especially dreaded as now I had to go against someone heavier than me, yet I won every time Coach Wellman moved me up out of my weight class. I was very proud to come through for the team and proud to receive Coach Wellman's pat on my back, especially because I rarely had any family supporting me at matches. My mom was a waitress and seamstress so was working a lot when I was wrestling, but she came when she could. My team became a family, and we went 11-1 losing only one dual to Worthington, Minnesota. But even though I had focus now, my crazy background still reared its head at times. During that dual against Worthington, the gym lights were dimmed so that the auditorium bleachers faded into blackness while a spotlight was trained on the center of the wrestling mat. This was frequently done at duals so the whole focus was on the wrestlers. There was no team to hide behind or anyone to blame for losing as a person could do in basketball if they wanted an excuse. There was a certain amount of pressure being under the spotlight that created anxiety. As the months and years wore on, I craved being in that spotlight knowing that now I was the one putting pressure on my opponent. On this night, the Worthington home crowd was in a frenzy, and some kids even threw popcorn at us when our team ran into the gymnasium for warm-ups and introductions before the start of the dual. It was pissing me off. At the conclusion of my match, while still under the spotlight, I gave the Worthington crowd the finger. Our team had one point deducted for unsportsmanlike conduct.

Coach Wellman shouted to the assistant coach, "Take him out and deal with him!"

The assistant grabbed me and hauled me to a back hallway where he choked me and chewed me out for five minutes. That wasn't the only time he had to deal with my temper, outbursts, or antics during my high school years. Another time before the start of an out-of-town wrestling meet, I told my varsity teammates that I was going to put my opponent on his back yet not pin him right away.

"I'll wave at you guys while I have this kid on his back. Then I'll pin him and wave at their home crowd."

I did just as I said I would, and the guys on my team got a big kick out of it. We lost a team point for unsportsmanlike conduct again, and I got hauled out of the gymnasium by the back of my neck. Our assistant coach put me up against the wall and chewed me out for a long time, telling me to get my behavior under control. His angry face was only an inch from mine.

"When you pull stuff like that the whole team suffers. This isn't just about you!"

It was just what I deserved and it was their way of trying to change my out-of-control behavior.

One of my teammates was a senior by the name of Randy Pascoe. Randy wasn't like many other people I'd known. He had good character, manners, discipline, and relentless determination.

We became good friends. When I would lose my temper, Randy would try to help me put things in perspective and calm me down. He was a star football player and a state champion in wrestling. Randy and I sat together on the bus on the way to wrestling meets and we often roomed together at tournaments. We had long talks on philosophical issues, and he would guide me like a mentor. Randy treated his girlfriend with respect, opened doors for her, and sent her cards and flowers. I'd never known anyone to do this before. I had a high school girlfriend, and he encouraged me to treat her with respect. Randy heard me mouth off to my mom one day. He didn't say anything at the time, but later on he told me to remember that she was a mom working hard at two jobs and had a difficult personal life. He told me to avoid arguing with her and to listen to her advice. No one had ever given me that perspective before. I began to follow his examples outwardly, yet inwardly I still had so much pent up anger. While the anger is what fueled me on to be a good, aggressive wrestler, it negatively affected my personal life. I would work myself into a frenzy before wrestling matches, pacing the floor, as I couldn't wait to get after my opponent. Teammates called me 'The Intimidator' yet it was no act. I enjoyed punishing opponents and being physically aggressive. Just to beat an opponent wasn't good enough. I wanted to hurt them and worked extra hard in practice on moves that were painful.

During my junior year I was undefeated and getting a lot of press. In the days before cable television, computers, iPads, and video games, people were entertained by following an athlete for something to do. I was ranked second in the state so my matches were being followed by the media. Well, that year they were also following an undefeated kid named Randy Lewis from Rapid City who was ranked first in the state. So, what excitement was in store as these two undefeated kids prepared to clash in the championship of a Sioux Falls tournament. There was a lot of hype building up to the match, and it seemed that's all I heard about from people at school and around town. All the hype ended quickly in that championship match as I wasn't even in Lewis's ballpark on the mat, but not because I wasn't tough. I was very tough, but I was inexperienced as a wrestler and had an opponent with years of intensive training. Lewis had been taken all over the country to wrestle as a youth and was trained at various camps and clinics. Many people made me feel bad about that loss like I'd let down the school and Sioux Falls as a whole. None of these people were aware of how sparse my wrestling background was or how experienced Randy Lewis was. I wasn't aware of it myself until many years later. But like everything in my life that was negative, I found a way to deal with it and move on. Incidentally, Lewis went on to become one of the greatest wrestlers our country has ever produced. Every year in high school he won state titles undefeated. He pinned forty-five opponents in a row, setting a national record. He won national championships for the famed Iowa Hawkeye wrestling program and went on to win an Olympic gold medal. Yes, he pinned me, but he also pinned 16 NCAA champions, four world and Olympic champions, and 17 world and Olympic medalists, so I consider myself in good company.

Despite losing to the great Randy Lewis, I finished my junior year successfully. I was chosen to represent the state of South Dakota on an all-star team that toured through the Midwest putting on wrestling exhibitions to raise money for charity. We wrestled against all-star teams from Iowa and Nebraska. Early into the tour we wrestled in Huron, South Dakota, which is a two hour drive from Sioux Falls. I was one of the light-weight wrestlers on the team so my match came up first. Less than a minute into my match I felt a strange pop in my knee and found that my leg was locked in a 90 degree angle. It wouldn't budge. I had to injury- default out of the match and was carried to a back room where trainers attempted to unlock my knee. They couldn't do it so instead packed my knee with ice and there I sat for two hours while my teammates wrestled. After that we had a two hour drive back home, and all this time I was sitting with my knee locked in that odd, uncomfortable position.

In the emergency room at the hospital, two doctors worked for half an hour attempting to unlock my knee but had no more success than the trainers. They injected my knee with dye and sent me for x-rays. As the doctors stood in the emergency room examining my x-rays, an older doctor with a cigarette hanging out the side of his mouth walked in. (That sure was a different time when a doctor was smoking in the hospital.)

"What do we have here," he mused, ash dropping to the floor from his cigarette.

He studied my x-rays for a minute, laid his cigarette on the edge of the counter top and walked over to me. With me lying on my back, he took hold of my leg and pushed my locked knee clear back by my ear. With my leg pushed as far as it would go, he twisted my foot hard to one side. My knee instantly unlocked. What a relief! The old veteran doctor accomplished in one minute what several medical people hadn't been able to do for hours.

The next week I went into the hospital for major surgery to repair my torn knee. The most vivid memory of that surgery is the morphine shots. Back then they managed pain differently. The nurse administered the first morphine hypo into my hip. Soon a warm feeling swept over me, and I felt like I was rising toward the ceiling. All my pain was gone, and I was content to float with this groggy high. Later I got a second shot which produced the same euphoria that's almost indescribable. I acted like I was in a lot of pain the next day in order to get more, but they wouldn't give me any. I know why pain is managed in a more controlled manner now as a person could easily get addicted to that kind of drug.

As I entered my senior year of wrestling, I cut from 132 lbs. down to 98 lbs. At the end of my senior year, I weighed in at 101 lbs on the final day at state due to a 3 lb. growth allowance during the year. After the tournament was over, we drove back across the state, and when we got back to our high school I weighed 115 lbs. When I graduated in May I was at 145. Kids aren't allowed to cut that much weight anymore, but at the time it was encouraged. I was issued a rubberized sweat suit as part of my wrestling gear. Now rubberized sweat suits are banned due to the dangers of heat exhaustion, and if a wrestler is caught using one, they are not allowed to compete the rest of that season. I never once failed to make weight and became furious when one of my teammates would let us down by not making weight. I cut so much weight that I lost my cool one day at school in our lunch room. We weighed in at 7:00 am for conference matches and this allowed us to eat during the day and wrestle at night. I had a school lunch, which for me was a rare thing. I had just sat down at my lunch table when a team mate who was not varsity and who cut no weight walked by and took some of my French fries stuffing them into his mouth. That was all it took, and my temper blew. I proceeded to pound that kid unmercifully right in the cafeteria. We were both hauled to the office for a visit to the discipline principal. I basically pled insanity due to severe hunger. I explained to our principal what had transpired and he knew how much weight I had cut. The principal yelled at that other kid for taking my French fries and I was allowed to go finish lunch. The principal let me wrestle that night and I served no school detention for the fight. I was doing good things for the high school, so that administrator just let it slide.

Time would eventually show that all the weight cutting was not a wise decision. Yes, I was undefeated, ranked #1 in the state and beat my Watertown opponent in the dual, who was ranked second in the state. He went on to win the state title that year at 98 lbs. with only one loss of the season: to me.

My failure to achieve a state title began over Christmas break of my senior year when I was severely burned. Cutting so much weight made me cold all the time so I would turn on the gas stove burners and use the fire to warm up. I stood too close one night, and my shirt caught on fire burning flesh and my shirt from my body. Most of my back, neck, and shoulders had severe burns. I was rushed to the hospital where these burns were numbed with medication, and the medical staff removed the burned flesh and shirt from my body. I could not feel the damaged skin being removed, but I could hear the sound it produced as charred flesh was pulled away. As they pulled the damaged skin off it sounded like someone ripping paper towels in half. The smell of my burned flesh was nauseating. I was told my wrestling was over for the season. I was devastated. I'd been on the road to a state title and so many cherished career records at my high school. After much debate following a 2 ½ week layoff, I was allowed to compete in competition by smearing a purple salve all over my burns and wearing a special burn shirt. I was not allowed to practice in the wrestling room due to infection risks. I could only run for conditioning and to keep my weight down. My wrestling edge was lost without the vital time needed in a wrestling room, and I did not achieve a state title as I lost two close matches at state. My losses were to opponents I'd beaten earlier in the year in close matches, so with my wrestling edge off it was their turn to win the close match. I ended up in 5th place which was extremely upsetting to me. But I did go on to accomplish many goals in high school. I was voted most promising underclassman by my teammates and coaches and in my senior year I was voted most valuable wrestler. I was captain of the team for two years. My records included most wins in a season, most team points scored in a season, most near-fall points in a season, quickest pin of the season, most wins in a career, and most team points scored in a career.

I was grateful that the doctors found a way for me to finish the season because, without their treatments, I wouldn't have accomplished a lot of those goals. Emotionally, though, it was a very upsetting finish to my high school wrestling career in which my main sight had been on a state championship.

The 11-1 team I was on my first year in high school. I was expected to perform at a high level even though I was the young guy in the lineup. I am in the back, far left. In front, far left is Randy Pascoe, the state champion, who taught me so much about good character and goals.

A special person in my life: Coach Ray Wellman. The team is hoisting him up following our section III championship. This was during my junior year. That team also went 11-1.

The much anticipated match-up as "the undefeated kid from Sioux Falls" (left), I go up against "the undefeated kid from Rapid City," Randy Lewis. He went on to win an Olympic Gold Medal in 1984. I am proud to have been on the same wrestling mat with him. We will stay in touch.

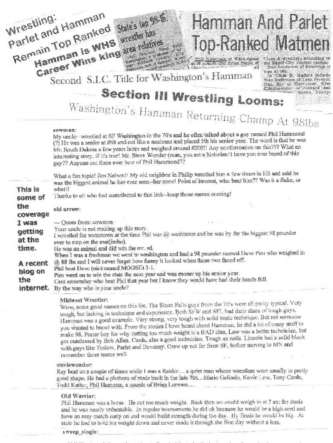

Wrestling:
Parlet and Hamman
Remain Top Ranked

State's top 98-lb.
wrestler has
area relatives

Hamman is WHS
Career Wins king

Hamman And Parlet
Top-Ranked Matmen

Second S.I.C. Title for Washington's Hamman

Section III Wrestling Looms:

Washington's Hamman Returning Champ At 98lbs

This is some of the coverage I was getting at the time.

A recent blog on the internet.

cowman:

My uncle wrestled at SF Washington in the 70's and he often talked about a guy named Phil Hammond (?) He was a senior at #98 and cut like a madman and placed 5th his senior year. The word is that he was Mr. South Dakota a few years later and weighed around #200!! Any conformation on this??? What an interesting story, if it's true! Mr. Steve Wonder (man, you are a historian!) have you ever heard of this guy?? Anyone out there ever hear of Phil Hammond??

What a fun topic! Jim Nelson!! My old neighbor in Philip wrestled him a few times in HS and said he was the biggest animal he has ever seen--bar none! Point of interest, who beat him?? Was it a fluke, or what!!

Thanks to all who had contributed to this link--keep those names coming!

old arrow:

— Quote from: cowman

Your uncle is not making up this story.

I wrestled for watertown at the time Phil was @ washinton and he was by far the biggest 98 pounder ever to step on the mat(imho).

He was an animal and did with the mr. sd.

When I was a freshman we went to washington and had a 98 pounder named Dave Piro who weighed in @ 88 lbs and I will never forget how funny it looked when those two faced off.

Phil beat Dave (nicknamed MOOSE) 3-1.

Piro went on to win the state the next year and was runner up his senior year.

Cant remember who beat Phil that year but I know they would have had their hands full.

By the way who is your uncle?

Midwest Wrestler:

Wow, some good names on this list. The Sioux Falls guys from the 70's were all pretty typical. Very tough, but lacking in technique and experience. Both SFW and SFL had their share of tough guys. Hamman was a good example. Very strong, very tough with solid basic technique. But not someone you wanted to brawl with. From the stories I have heard about Hamman, he did a lot of crazy stuff to make 98. Poster boy for why cutting too much weight is a BAD idea. Law was a better technician, but got outclassed by Bob Allen. Carda, also a good technician. Tough as nails. Lincoln had a solid block with guys like Teslow, Parlet and Devanny. Grew up not far from SF, before moving to MN and remember those teams well.

steviewonder:

Ray beat us a couple of times while I was a Raider.... a quiet man whose wrestlers were usually in pretty good shape. He had a plethora of studs back in the late 70's....Mario Galindo, Kevin Law, Tony Carda, Todd Kutter, Phil Hamman, a couple of Brian Larsons....

Old Warrior:

Phil Hamman was a horse. He cut too much weight. Back then we could weigh in at 7 am for duals and he was nearly unbeatable. In regular tournaments he did ok because he would be a high seed and have an easy match early on and would build strength during the day. By finals he would be big. At state he had to hold his weight down and never made it through the first day without a loss.

sweep_single:

Phil Hammond also got booted out of south dakota for the longest time for getting into so many bar brawls, thats why he is/was the head coach of sioux city.

Dark Times

After all the difficulties I'd overcome as a child, I entered an even darker time after high school. My life started to spiral out of control. Various college coaches had contacted me to wrestle, and I was offered a scholarship to a college in the next state. I declined when my girlfriend did not want me to leave town. Instead I chose a college nearby in part because the head wrestling coach had lived through a tough childhood like me so we bonded. I was still distraught over my upsetting high school wrestling finish. My place on the Washington wrestling team was filled by new shoes, and everyone moved on, but I missed the connection I'd felt with my teammates. Now, at college, I was not able to make the starting line-up as the team was loaded with excellent upperclassmen. To make the line-up the next season, I knew I'd need to cut nearly twenty pounds which was not what I wanted to do. The most devastating event was the end of a long relationship with my high school girlfriend, especially after I'd given up a college scholarship to stay near her. She'd started drinking, partying, and making a lot of other bad choices. I didn't want to go down that road and thought I could convince her to change. I wanted to continue down my own new path as I'd set new goals that involved college and athletics. Even though she had no future goals, and we'd ended up on completely different tracks, I was desperate to convince her to change. She'd given me a sense of security that I craved. Many times, she'd been the only one who came to support me at a wrestling meet. She had an intact family that did things together, and they included me in their family circle. It was something I'd never experienced and emotionally needed. In a matter of minutes, she left and all that security was gone. I felt empty and depressed. Now I was alone much of the time as I didn't have my girlfriend, and my mom was never around. Loneliness and grief started fueling my anger, and my thinking became irrational.

Randy Pascoe had moved away, too. All the values he'd taught me about good character, treating women with respect, and living a decent life began to fade away, becoming lost in the shadows of grief. I started thinking that his advice and my coach's advice were all bullshit.

Their ideas hadn't gotten me anywhere, and I lost my girlfriend even when I had been treating her well. Falling back on the familiar, I regressed to my Norton-Froehlich mentality. Disgusted with everything and everyone, I walked away from college after a year and went to work at a meat-packing plant. I started hanging out with old friends who frequented rough places and lived in appalling situations. I weighed 200 lbs., squatted 460 lbs., and bench pressed 360 lbs. I was 'The Intimidator' again. I had grown up fist fighting and I had just spent years on a wrestling mat. This group of friends I was constantly with were hardcore street guys. We were continually getting in fist fights and doing illegal things. It didn't take us long to build up a reputation as guys who were not to be messed with. This was ultimate fighting with no rules, no tapping out, and no referee to keep a person from being killed in a street brawl. My old strategy of dealing with my pain by inflicting pain on others crept back to replace the new values I'd abandoned. I was off the path. During this dark time, I reached a point where I just didn't care what happened, and when you deal with someone who doesn't care, you're dealing with trouble.

Mr. I

Throughout this dark time, I easily could have been killed. In my state of not caring about anything, I was frequenting rough establishments where violent people were not only intoxicated but most likely carried weapons, too. Being an excellent billiard player and having won many big tournaments, I often hustled pool to earn some extra money. The individuals who filled these places were easy targets from whom I could almost always win a few bucks. However, when you mix alcohol with people losing their money, it adds up to trouble. Over the years, many businesses have removed their pool tables due to all the fights and damage caused by bad shots and lost games.

My longtime friend, Mr. I, was alongside me during many dangerous confrontations. Doug Wallin's nickname 'Mr. I stood for Mr. Irritable because his quick, violent temper could flare up at any seemingly mild irritation. Standing 6' 1" and 235 pounds, he was someone I could always, and I mean always, count on if a situation turned dangerous. He had piercing eyes that, when angry, would seem to bore holes in a person. Whenever I saw those angry eyes lock onto somebody I knew that person was in deep trouble and would more than likely be taking a trip to the hospital or dentist. Mr. I could unleash some of the most devastating punches I've ever seen thrown in a fist fight. These punches broke jaws, shattered cheek bones, broke noses, and knocked the teeth out of several people.

Doug was a starting player on one of our undefeated high school football teams. At Washington High, a school which holds a national record for the most state football championships, being a starting player could change your whole future, because it was likely that college coaches would be talking to you. Unfortunately, due to personal family problems, Doug dropped out of school, which ended his potentially bright athletic future.

Doug and I had a philosophy when we went out on the town. That philosophy was that we weren't going to give anybody any crap, but we weren't going to take any crap from anybody either. Women

81

weren't exempt from this philosophy. If a woman wanted to be treated with respect, she needed to act respectfully, and if she wanted to fight like a man she'd be treated like a man. A fine example of putting this philosophy into practice happened at a house party one evening. Doug was in an argument with a guy as they stood on the back deck. The guy's girlfriend came up and spit in Mr. I's face. That was the wrong thing to do. Without hesitation, Mr. I unleashed one of those fearsome punches right in her face. She flew backwards down a flight of twelve stairs and was knocked unconscious. When she got out of the hospital she filed a civil lawsuit against Mr. I because she'd hurt her back and neck. Doug was found not guilty because she'd been in another fight earlier that evening and couldn't prove when she'd sustained the injuries. A good lawyer is worth his weight in gold.

There was a motorcycle gang in the area, and my group of friends and I had on-going fist fights with them every other weekend. These bikers were used to going around and intimidating people with their numbers and their tough-guy acts. Don't get me wrong; some of these bikers were as rough and tough as anybody, but most of them were only tough when their buddies were there to back them up. It all started when one of these bikers, dressed in full colors, was watching Mr. I and me play pool. He mouthed off something and right away I saw Mr. I lock his angry eyes onto that biker.

"Listen, you dirty creep, just because you grow a beard, wear grungy leathers, and act tough, doesn't mean you're tough. How come you dirtballs have to dress up like it's Halloween every time you go out? Say ONE more word to me, and I'll come across this pool room and show everyone in here how tough you aren't."

The biker hung his head. He knew Mr. I meant business. His usual intimidation wasn't working here. But after this incident, every time we ran into this group of bikers, a fight broke out. We never backed down even when outnumbered. One night my friends and I were in a particularly rough joint called the Frontier Club. Right as we were walking out, guess who walked in: about seven members of the biker gang. In an instant, there were ten people all fist fighting which spilled out the door and onto the street. The fight was violent and didn't seem like it was going to end. During the course of this fight, I was grabbed from behind in a strong choke hold. Thinking that a biker had me from behind, I crouched low, reached back and got a hold of the person by the shirt, I then flipped this person over my shoulder onto the sidewalk in front of me. To my shock, it was a police officer who hit the ground. Unbeknownst to me, several patrol cars had pulled up during the fight. Three other officers grabbed a hold of me and started dragging me toward a squad car. I was trying to explain to them that I didn't know it was a police officer I'd thrown on the ground. They were in no mood to listen and started hitting me with billy clubs instead. In the process, one of the officers broke my elbow. Along with me, two of my friends also went to jail, but none of the bikers were arrested which didn't seem right to us, but we got a little satisfaction knowing two of them went to the hospital. I got the worst of it as I visited both the police station and hospital. That night I was able to bail out of jail and went to the emergency room where they put a cast on my arm. When my friends and I went in front of the judge the next week, we lucked out and got a judge who knew us, was a wise man, and who knew those bikers were a lot of trouble around town.

He told us, "So, it was you boys who got half the police department to work on Saturday night." He then spoke to me, "Mr. Hamman, tell me about this police officer getting thrown on the ground."

I explained my version to him, and then he asked what happened to my arm.

I said, "Three other cops grabbed me and hit me with billy clubs and broke my arm."

The judge smiled and said, "Well, we'll call that even then."

He told us to stay out of trouble, and that he didn't want to keep seeing us in his court room. Then he let us slide with disorderly conduct and a $100 fine each. In the 70's, fist fights were much more common and not considered such a big deal like they are now. Cops often just broke up fights and told people to go home. If someone was charged, it was usually a misdemeanor which is in the same category as traffic violations.

Eventually the biker gang disappeared from town after one of the members shot and killed a guy in a club across town. A friend of mine, who later ended up being the singer in my wedding, was the drummer for the band that was playing in the club the night of the shooting. When he heard the pop of the gun, he thought the sound came from him accidentally hitting the rim of his drum. Anyway, the cops cracked down on the whole group of bikers and ran them out of town after they shot and killed that guy.

There's an old saying, "There never was a horse that couldn't be rode, and there's never been a rider that couldn't be throwed." So, if someone wants to go out and fist fight, he'd better be ready to get a butt-kicking eventually. At the first annual Sioux Falls street dance, there were three bands playing and about 8,000 people in attendance. I got together with Mr. I and a group of friends to go check it out. The crowd danced while one of the bands performed one of Bob Seger's hits.

At around midnight, I was talking to some people I knew and had gotten separated from Mr. I. One of my friends came running up and said, "Mr. I got in a fight! We have to get over there fast."

When we got to where he was, there was a whole crowd of people standing around including police officers. When I saw Mr. I, I couldn't believe it. I almost didn't recognize him. He didn't even look human. Both of his eyes were swollen almost completely closed. His lips were severely bloodied and puffed out. He had all kinds of other welts and marks on his head. There were lumps and contusions of all sizes covering his face that were already turning black and blue. He was a bloody mess. What had happened was that he'd gotten into a fight with eight college football players. They had ganged up on him, and when he fell on his hands and knees, they circled him and kicked him repeatedly in the face.

Mr. I could barely stand up. He was actually holding onto a police officer to stay steady. Standing in front of him was one of the football players, a large young man about 6' 3" and 250 lbs. In a very calm voice, Mr. I said to this football player, "Yeah, you guys kicked my ass good, and I have to go to the hospital. But I remember you, big guy, hitting and kicking me, so before I go to the hospital . . . you get this!" From somewhere deep within, Mr. I summoned the strength to kick the guy, harder than I've ever seen anybody get kicked, and he got him right in the privates. This football player grabbed himself, let out a shriek, and fell to the ground where he curled into the fetal position. That kick almost started another fight, but the police were right there and stopped it. One of the other football players said to an officer, "You saw what he just did. Arrest him!" The police officer replied, "Are you kidding? Look at what you guys did to him. He has to go to the hospital." With that, the police made everyone clear out, and we left to take Mr. I to the hospital. By the time we'd walked to our car five minutes later, I looked back and the football player who had been kicked was still curled up on the ground in a fetal position. Even after being beaten almost unconscious, it didn't stop the 'Mr. I' in him from coming out to get some final revenge.

Mr. I was definitely someone you did not steal from without facing dire consequences. At one time, Doug was living in a trailer park and had a neighbor who came over frequently to hang out and watch TV. This neighbor had a buddy living with him who was a transient and was homeless at the time. The transient, therefore, spent some time at Doug's home as well. It so happened that Doug needed to go out of town for two weeks, and upon his return he discovered that his home had been burglarized. Many items including his shotgun, fishing gear, stereo, and some jewelry had been stolen. Whoever had burglarized the home knew that Doug would not be back for some time as they had slept in his bed, eaten all the food in the refrigerator, and left dirty dishes all over. Upon checking with his neighbor, Doug discovered that the transient had left about the same time Doug had left town, and had sold Doug's fishing pole to this neighbor who was unaware it belonged to Doug. After hearing this, Doug transformed into Mr. I, and he set out to find the burglar. Unfortunately, nobody knew where the transient had gone. He continued to hunt for the guy for over a week with no success when one day good luck struck for Mr. I, which was bad luck for the thief.

Wilbur, who was another longtime friend of ours, was headed down the highway with Mr. I, when to their total surprise and delight, they saw the burglar hitchhiking down the highway! Mr. I was driving, and he told Wilbur, "I'll keep my head turned away so he won't recognize me. Offer him a ride, and when he gets into the backseat, you hop back there and hold him." Wilbur was a tough guy himself, and when this hitchhiking burglar got into the backseat, Wilbur had him. They said that a look of terror crossed his face when he realized Mr. I was driving. They took the thief back to Mr. I's trailer where they beat him up for a while. Then they made him strip off all his clothes except for his underwear. It was winter and there was snow on the ground so with no clothes or shoes, Mr. I felt the burglar had less chance to escape. As punishment, they made him clean the whole house and do all the dirty dishes. They'd hit him while he was in the process of vacuuming and doing all the laundry. Wilbur and Mr. I figured that if the guy went to the police about this kidnapping that it would be the transient's story against their concocted version of what happened. Also, the transient would face burglary charges that could be proven. After the thief had completed all the household chores, he was placed in the backseat of Mr. I's car with Wilbur holding him. The thief was still clad only in his underwear but was given a blanket to wrap up in. Next, Mr. I had the burglar direct him to the various locations where the stolen goods had been sold, and he talked to the people who'd bought these items. Mr. I would point to the thief sitting in the backseat and say, "See that creep in my car? He broke into my home and what you bought from him, I want back." Mr. I recovered 90% of his possessions except for some jewelry that went to a pawn shop and had been immediately sold. The process to recover all the goods took two days, so the thief had to be held overnight. To do this, Mr. I put the transient in a back bedroom of his trailer home. The one small window in the bedroom was broken and would not open so there would be no way for him to escape through it. Then he had to be prevented from sneaking out after Mr. I fell asleep. Wilbur pulled the couch down the hallway of the trailer, put the thief in the rear bedroom, and pushed the couch against the bedroom door thereby locking the captor inside. Mr. I slept on the couch to ensure no escape was possible. The thief was given no food but was given a coffee can for a chamber pot at night. After two days, the transient was finally given all his clothes except for his socks and shoes. He was made to run off through the snow barefoot. Mr. I found out later that he'd had to run three blocks until reaching a friend's house, and he had suffered mild frostbite on both feet in the process. But as Mr. I figured, he did not report the incident to the authorities.

Reputation

It was still like the Wild West, in a sense, when I was with my buddies running the streets in the 1970's. Our society had not cracked down on domestic violence, bullying in schools, fire arms, drunk driving, or fist fighting. We were fighting all the time, and my reputation as a street fighter grew immensely one night. I was with Mr. I., Chuck (who'd been shot by the little kid), and Wilbur (who'd helped Mr. I kidnap the thief.) We decided to go to a known biker gang club because we'd heard that someone we knew was bartending there. This place had a bouncer named Giovanni who had a reputation as a bad dude. Giovanni was a big, mean Italian, standing 6'2" and 240 lbs. with a crooked broken nose. We were only going to check this club out and had no intention of trouble. We were all still young, about 21 years old and obviously not very wise yet. We had yet to learn that when you put yourself in a bad environment, something bad is bound to happen. The place was crowded and toward closing time, Chuck and Wilbur were talking to a couple of girls. Apparently Giovanni did not like this and told them to take a hike. They came and found me, so we all went outside of the bar at closing time where many of the patrons had gathered on the front of the sidewalk to talk before leaving. As we stood out there in this crowd of people, Giovanni, along with some bikers, went up to Chuck. Giovanni poked Chuck in the chest and said, "Beat it. I want you out of my sight." He then moved to Wilbur, poked him in the chest and told Wilbur the same thing. It was intimidation and a way to humiliate us in front of a crowd. I remember exactly, to this day, what I said to Mr. I. "If this guy comes over to us and puts his hands on me, I'm letting him have it. Just don't let him kill me." Sure enough, this bouncer stepped over to me and said, "You guys beat it, too." He hadn't touched me, but it was still intimidation. I said, "You don't own the sidewalk. We can be out here." Giovanni turned, poked me in the chest, and said, "I'll own *you*." *Wham.* I hit him with every bit of strength I could muster. Giovanni's head snapped back and he was left with a huge gash above his eye. Without hesitating, he grabbed me and we flew out into the street and onto the ground, both trying to gain control of the other person. On the ground, though, I was in my element. I was the wrestler; I had an edge by not being on my feet going toe to toe with him. I maneuvered myself in front of Giovanni and applied a front choke hold. In a wrestling match, this is illegal, but it is a Jui Jitsu strangulation move. My forearm was across his trachea, and I locked on, applying the choke. I remained locked like a pit bull and just waited for the choke to start taking effect. In his desperation, Giovanni pushed me up against a parked car. He was so big and strong that he actually started lifting me up off the ground while I was still applying the hold. I knew he'd have a standing advantage, so as I came off the ground I hooked my heels into the wheel well of the parked car, keeping him from lifting me further. We stayed stuck in this position, and I kept squeezing the strangulation hold with all my strength. In this position, I was able to look around and could see Mr. I., Chuck, and Wilbur fighting with the guys who were with Giovanni. After two long minutes, I felt Giovanni getting weak, and he softly gagged out, "Let me go." I was not convinced and did not let up since this guy had a bad reputation.

A door slammed, the crowd parted, and Charlie Johnston, a huge, burly bartender from the club, came out and yelled, "Phil, stop the fighting. We don't want cops coming here." Charlie knew me from watching me wrestle while I was in high school. He had followed our team closely and was a big Washington High Athletic booster. All of us stopped fighting and when I let Giovanni go, I was covered in blood from the huge gash in his brow line. Giovanni told Charlie that we had jumped them unexpectedly. I said, "That is crap, Charlie. If your bouncer wants to go out back, I'll give him a second go." People yelled for Giovanni to go fight, but he hung his head and said no. Now it was Giovanni who had been humiliated. My body was hopped up on adrenaline, but we had to clear out of the place. We started to leave but people kept coming up and congratulating me, patting me on the back, and I could hear the crowd buzzing about seeing the bad- ass bouncer get beat up. The satisfaction was short lived. This reputation just caused more trouble because other tough guys around would challenge me or my friends. I had many other fights and I never lost one of them. After the incident with Giovanni, a couple of clubs told us we couldn't come in there because of our reputation. It was a dark time.

Bouncer Blues

Even my job put me in risky situations at times. I was working as a bouncer in a rough club downtown. Besides having to deal with the routine problems each night such as drunken patrons, fighting, or enforcing the dress code, which included: no gang colors, no muscle shirts, and no hats. Hats actually cause a lot of problems in a bar. People will knock a hat off someone or cowboys wearing their hats tend to get wilder. "Yee Haw" gets louder with each shot of whiskey. The job got more difficult once a month when the owners hired strippers from Minneapolis or Kansas City to perform on a stage in the rear of the club. So, as dancers gyrated to The Rolling Stones' *Honky Tonk Woman,* I kicked men out for getting too touchy-feely. These strippers not only performed on stage but arranged for work after hours with our customers. Many of the girls were hardcore drug abusers who would literally sell their kids for that white line. The strippers would drive into town with their pimps.

One night I had to check our back parking lot, and in the back seat of a car was one of the strippers engaged in sexual acts, presumably for money. She was doing this while her six-year-old child was sleeping in the front seat. It really pissed me off. I knocked on the rear window when next to me a harsh voice said, "Hey, chump, you best go back inside and do your job." It was her pimp. I said, "Conduct in our parking lot is part of my job, chump." He stuck his hand in his pocket like he had a gun and replied, "Get back inside; it's the last time I'm tellin' ya." I went into the club and called the police, but the pimp and his stripper were gone by the time they arrived.

The job became the most difficult when our club owners brought in the male strippers. Those women must have really needed to cut loose when they got the chance to go out on the town because we had more fights, arrests, and violence when the club was full of intoxicated females. The male strippers included: The turban-wearing Genie Man who performed his strip act on a magic carpet (lambskin rug) on the stage, the Phantom of the Opera who wore a mask and long cape, and the Lone Ranger and Tonto, one dressed like a cowboy and his partner in a politically incorrect Native American-style breechcloth and feathers. During the performances, drunk women would hop on the stage to grab the male strippers, or they would start stripping themselves. When I would grab them to pull them off the stage, they would hit, kick, and scratch me. Also, no men were allowed in the club on these nights as it was advertised as female admittance only. Jealous husbands and boyfriends would show up demanding entrance so they could remove their women, and fights occurred often at the front entrance of the club. It was dysfunctional.

The Starlight Drive-In

Another job I had around this time in my life was working as one of the security employees at the Starlight Theater. Drive-in movies were very popular at the time, and the theater was often packed with customers watching the movie from their vehicles, drinking alcohol, making out with their dates, and eating a variety of popular concession stand food which included popcorn, foot long chili dogs, cotton candy, giant dill pickles, and pizza. My job involved breaking up fights, disorderly drinking parties, and watching for people sneaking into the theater by scaling the 8-foot wooden fence that surrounded the perimeter of the theater grounds. The theater was comprised of a huge gravel lot with a speaker pole marking each parking spot. A car would pull up alongside the speaker, which was attached to a 4-foot wire so it could be placed inside the vehicle. On weekends, cars would line up for blocks to purchase tickets. I would watch for vehicles in line that hung low in the rear of the car. This indicated that there were people hiding in the trunk so they didn't have to pay. These low-riding cars usually had just a driver in the front of the car. The drive-in was only open in the summers, so it was usually very hot and the stowaways in the trunk would be suffering in there. Sometimes I could hear the people yell to the driver, "How much longer? We can't breathe in here!" The driver would respond with, "Shut up. Security is right up ahead." I would let these low-riders wait in line until they got right up to the ticket booth and then I would tell the driver to pull out of line and open the trunk. They would always complain and ask why, and I would say, "I think you have people in the trunk." When the trunk was finally opened, there would be anywhere from two to five stowaways lying inside. As the embarrassed culprits exited the trunk, the other cars in line would honk their horns and yell things like, "Cheapskates!"

At the end of the night when the movies concluded, there would always be some cars left in the lot long after all the other patrons had left. My job was to clear out these last vehicles so the gates could be locked. The leftover vehicles usually belonged to people who were passed out from drinking too much or because their car was unable to start due to a dead battery. There was a two-wheeled cart that held a battery pack and jump start cables if a car needed a jump start. One evening, another security employee and I walked up to a vehicle still on the lot. There was an old guy inside who looked to be 70 years old. He had a huge, bushy beard, looked like a hermit, and was passed out. There must have been a case of empty beer cans strewn about the inside of the car. His window was half down, and we decided to have a little fun, as we often did, getting the guy to leave. I leaned in right next to his ear and yelled, "Get the hell out of here! The movie's over!" The guy startled awake, turned on his ignition, and roared off, half awake, through the lot like a crazy man. He was going at least 50 mph and hitting speaker poles as he sped along breaking them off at ground level. He was headed right at the big wooden perimeter fence. The guy with me said, "Oh, no! He's going to smash through the fence!" Sure enough, he hit that fence at a high speed, knocking a gaping hole twenty feet wide and sending wood flying into the air in all directions. I couldn't believe it. The last we saw of the old guy's car was its red taillights bouncing off in the distance as he drove across a long pasture that bordered the drive-in. The manager came out of the concessions building yelling, "What was that crash I just heard?" I told the manager that a guy was passed out, and I politely asked him to leave, but he went crazy and crashed through the fence.

At the same time I was working at the drive-in, I was also working at a restaurant. One of the managers was a weird guy who I nicknamed Creepster. He was about 35 years old, married, and had children. Creepster would always come out to the drive-in theater and try touching the teenage girls who would hang out and talk to me. He also lived in an apartment complex and would ask the girls to go take a Jacuzzi with him there, while mentioning that he had access to other apartments and suggesting sexual activities. Women didn't have much recourse for sexual harassment in those days.

Creepster had beady little eyes, a pot belly, and was balding, so of course these young, pretty girls would brush him off. Then he'd get mad at me and the next day at work would order me to do all kinds of undesirable jobs like cleaning grease traps and toilets. I had a real knack for turning the tables on people who got on my bad side. I decided to get him in a fix that would give me control. Shelly was a girl I knew who was pretty, full-figured, and liked me since I hung out with her brothers. A buddy of mine owned a customized van with a bed in the back which I knew would be perfect for my plan. I told Shelly about the slime ball manager and explained my plan to blackmail him. "Shelly, you just get him in on the bed in the van, and I'll step in and take a photo of him with you. That's all you'd need to do." Shelly agreed and we made a plan to execute my scheme the following Saturday night. I set up Creepster by telling him I knew of a wild teenage girl who liked older guys. I also told him she'd be at the drive-in Saturday night having a van drinking party. "Why don't you stop at the van party and see what transpires," I slyly suggested to him. Like a fish to bait, he went for it hook, line, and sinker, and came to the van with me that Saturday night. Shelly played it perfectly. I think she could have won an Oscar. She hung around with Creepster, then put her arm around him, taking him into the van. *Flash.* The camera went off, and Shelly pushed him away. I had him now. I then told him if he didn't meet my demands I would send the photo to his wife along with a letter telling her everything he had been doing. He got very worried and said he'd do what I wanted. "Just don't send that photo to my wife," he said with genuine concern in his voice. My demands were: all my buddies got free food, I got to pick all my own hours and job assignments, and I never had to clean grease traps or toilets. I followed through with my demands, too. When my buddies would come and eat tons of free food, the manager would just stand there looking angry, but he never said a word. I landed a job that paid better, so I quit that restaurant job at the end of the summer.

The ironic part is, the photo I took never turned out. Something was wrong with the camera and all the photos were black. Creepster, however, thought the photo existed of him being unfaithful to his wife.

Matthew

Having been arrested 42 times, charged with multiple felonies, served four different sentences in the state penitentiary, suffered five broken hands from street fights, stabbed, outran the law in high-speed chases numerous times, and a longtime friend of mine since we were young, Matt Lofton is a unique individual. Matt scored over 130 when given an IQ test during one of his prison stretches, so the associate warden called him into the office and offered to get Matt enrolled in a college upon his parole. Yet because of his difficult childhood, Matt was living a dysfunctional life and using his intelligence to carry out deviant scams instead.

One example of this was Matt's 'till tap scam' which he used to get extra money. The till tap worked like this: Matt would target a full service gas station with only one employee on duty. He'd walk into the gas station and ask the attendant for change for the pop machine or to use the pay phone. When the attendant opened the till to get the change, Matt would look to see which button was pushed to open the cash drawer. Then, Matt would linger in the station drinking his pop or pretending to use the phone. When a customer or one of Matt's accomplices drove into the station for full service, the attendant would go outside which allowed Matt to quickly make his move. Stepping to the cash register, Matt would 'tap the till' causing the drawer to open. Then he'd snatch a few ten and twenty dollar bills. He was careful not to clean out the drawer, so the bills weren't missed until the money was totaled at the end of the night. This scam worked 100% of the time for many years until video surveillance cameras became standard equipment in these establishments.

When self-serve gas stations sprang up around the country, Matt didn't pay for gas for years. He'd dust up the license plates on his car, wear a hat and dark glasses to conceal his identity, fill up his tank, and leave. All he had to do was rotate gas stations. My friends and I had been getting in a lot of trouble, and I decided to see if getting away to

California and staying with a friend for a while would help my situation. Matt decided he wanted to follow me out to Los Angeles to see what it was like. He drove separately because he wasn't sure if he'd like it or whether he'd want to stay. On the way out, I paid for my gas while Matt pulled his self-serve scam the whole way there and back. The only exception was that in L.A., they must have been used to this scam because the gas stations there posted an employee by the pumps.

Our trip to Los Angeles didn't last long. Everything was expensive, and it was too crowded, so we found ourselves back in Sioux Falls getting into as much trouble as ever. What started as an argument over a billiards game led to an ongoing fight with a group of four brothers who were from, of all places, Norton-Froehlich. Every time we ran into these brothers, a fight would break out. During these fights, I suffered two broken hands from punching people and a broken nose, which happened to be my third broken nose as it had been broken twice in wrestling. The clash with these brothers came to a climax late one night when we ran into them at a house party. It didn't take two seconds before a nine-person brawl erupted outside the house. One of the brothers grabbed a shotgun out of his vehicle and shot and wounded one of my friends with buckshot. Another of my buddies tackled the shotgun-wielding foe before he could get any more shots off and then beat the guy unconscious. My buddy then broke the shotgun to pieces by slamming it repeatedly on the street. Matt was on the ground in the middle of the street fighting with one of those brothers when the fourth brother hopped into a pickup truck, and in his panic to escape this brawl, ran over his own brother and Matt who were both still in the street. The fight went on for a long time and the violence kept escalating.

Eventually a deputy sheriff, highway patrol, and two ambulances showed up. Four people were taken to the hospital. Matt had a dislocated hip, broken bones, and internal injuries. Another victim had to have buckshot removed from various parts of his body, and another brother had a severe concussion. In addition, the shooter who was unconscious remained in a coma for two days. We were all fortunate that no one was killed. Even in court, the charges were surprisingly mild except for the aggravated assault charge against the shooter who incidentally got the charges dropped. His lawyer claimed self-defense due to the violent nature of the fight. The shooter had another lawyer that was worth his weight in gold.

Weeks later, Matt and I were leaving a pool hall at the end of the night when Matt drove through a stop sign without even slowing down. Coming down the street perpendicular to us was a police car, and the officer had seen Matt's blatant traffic violation. We saw the red lights start blinking and Matt hit the gas pedal. He was out past his court-ordered curfew which would mean a parole violation so he was desperate to get away. I could hear the sirens wailing as Matt accelerated quickly and turned off his headlights to make the car harder to see. So, we were careening down side streets in darkness at speeds up to 100 mph. Occasionally, Matt would slam on his brakes, turn down a different street, and race back to 100 mph. I was so nervous, and I kept yelling for Matt to slow down and be careful, but we just kept going faster. The cop started falling farther behind. When Matt was able to turn a corner completely out of sight with the cop car six blocks behind us, he pulled into a long, hedge-lined driveway and shut off the car. It worked, and the patrol car shot past us and disappeared into the night. My heart was racing, and I leaned my head against the door of the car letting out a sigh of relief. Leaving the lights off, Matt headed down back alleys until we were into a completely different part of town. He was elated at his successful escape, but we knew we were fortunate we hadn't been killed or hit another car full of innocent people.

That wasn't our only mishap involving a car. Matt was driving us to a club where we often played pool. This club was on a hill, so there was an elevated parking lot on one side with the club's front door down on the street level. Matt came roaring into the elevated lot going about 40 mph. The lot was icy, and Matt couldn't slow down. The car barreled over the perimeter barricade which consisted of railroad ties and a chain link fence. Busting through the fence we flew off the 8-foot wall and landed on the headlights of the car. By another stroke of luck, the car did not flip over onto its roof but balanced momentarily on the front end until the rear end fell back against the wall. The vehicle then stood awkwardly in a vertical position leaning against the wall. Since we weren't wearing seat belts, we were thrown into the dash and windshield. Shaken, but not seriously injured, both of us crawled out of the side doors. Nobody saw us exit the car, but within seconds there was a crowd of 100 people who'd trickled out of the club to see the bizarre wreck. Matt and I mingled with the crowd, and looked around seemingly as puzzled as everyone else when the club's owner came out yelling, "Who was driving that car?" Soon, a cop showed up and walked around asking who had seen the driver of the car. Then two tow trucks arrived on the scene, one above in the elevated parking lot and one below. With much effort, the two trucks were able to hoist Matt's car up to the top. Matt had disappeared from the crowd, and I figured he'd taken off upon the arrival of the cop. A few minutes later, Matt came up to me and said, "Phil, you won't believe it, my car has a lot of damage but still runs and nobody is up on the top lot with it." We snuck around the club and entered the elevated lot from a dark alley. Still, no one was up there, so we hopped in Matt's car and took off. We got away with it, too. Apparently, nobody had written down the license plate number of the car. Unbelievable!

One example of how out-of-control we were during this time occurred one night when we were out hustling pool. Matt, Doug, and I got into a fight, and Matt was arrested around 10:00 PM. Doug and I got bail money together and went to the county jail to get Matt released. We were back on the town by 11:30 PM. About 1:00 AM we were involved in another brawl, and Matt was arrested for the second time in the same evening.

Matt continued to develop and perfect increasingly sophisticated scams over the years. He was caught on several occasions but got away with a lot, too. *Brrrrrriiinngg.* I answered my phone and heard Matt's brother on the other line. "Phil, I'm just letting you know that this afternoon Matt outran a deputy sheriff in a high speed chase. He has a pistol and says he'd rather shoot it out than go back to the pen." My mind raced around thinking a hundred thoughts. I knew Matt had a felony warrant out for his arrest. He was being charged with selling stolen goods. He had traded marijuana for stolen goods and then sold the stolen goods for cash. Someone along the lines got caught and gave the police Matt's name in exchange for a lighter sentence.

Two nights later, my phone rang again, and it was Matt. "Phil, I'm coming over to your place. "

"No," I responded, "do you still have the handgun?" He said that he had it on him right at that moment. I told him he couldn't come to my place, but that I'd meet him in the parking lot of a business that we both agreed would be a discreet place. My plan was to talk him into giving me the handgun so there wouldn't be a shoot-out. I figured I had a 50-50 chance of success. We met, but he refused to hand over the pistol. He gave me a hug and told me he was going to head into a big city, change his identity, and lay low for a while. He said he'd get a hold of me sometime in the future. After all the years of Matt's crazy escapades I didn't think anything involving Matt would surprise me. None of us expected what his future actually held.

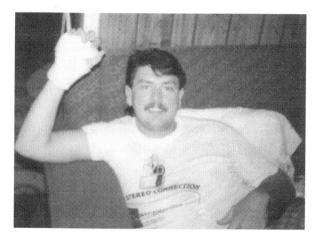

Mr. I sporting a broken hand after he'd "dished it out" to someone...

...sporting a black eye after someone "dished it out" to him.

Matt and I in Las Vegas on the trip to California where Matt didn't pay for any gas the whole trip.

Me, on Halloween, dressed like a thug, and—at the time—acting like one.

Steve and Uncle Allen

Steve Joslyn has been like a brother to me over the years ever since we met at a junior high wrestling tournament. Both of us liked to hunt, so it's no surprise that we somehow gravitated toward each other that day and spent time between wrestling matches talking. Steve went to a different junior high and hadn't been exposed to the violence that permeated my school. He also lived in one of the nice parts of town and hadn't been poisoned by poverty or an abusive childhood. His mother was loving and intelligent, and made sure that Steve was well-read so that he became intelligent, too. I've always been amazed by Steve's ability to talk in-depth about any topic that arises. His mom, who we jokingly called Big Kay, stood right at five feet tall and owned a used bookstore. Every time her store had to switch locations or she bought a big lot of books, she called on Steve and me to cart those ungodly heavy and dusty boxes of books around. She always treated me well and offered me things to eat. When she went to Steve's wrestling matches, she'd always come over and give me a compliment, too. Steve, much like Randy Pascoe, always tried to be the voice of reason with me over the years. I recall him often saying, "Phil, just walk away. A fight isn't worth the problems." But my anger usually got the best of me and, sadly, I sometimes even turned my anger on Steve when he tried to intervene. I'd yell and tell him to mind his own business, but being a good friend, he had the ability to understand where I was coming from and kept encouraging me to make better choices by his own example. Years later, it was Steve who encouraged me to use my weightlifting for constructive purposes. He worked out with me faithfully when I started competing in power lifting and bodybuilding competitions and was my work-out partner while I trained, and I eventually won the Mr. South Dakota Bodybuilding Contest. Steve also had his own life to get in order, though. He went away to college and wasn't around much of the time during those years when I was struggling the most.

Besides Steve, my uncles and aunts on my mom's side made efforts to try to do things for me and help my mom financially. But, I didn't live with them, so their influence wasn't the dominant factor in my life, unfortunately. Teachers see the same thing happen in schools. They try to influence their students, but those who return to dysfunctional home lives at the end of the day are met with a more powerful force than any positive messages given at school.

My uncle Allen, who was a police officer, was the closest thing I had to a father. When I was about ten years old, he'd let me ride around in the police car with him before regulations were put into place prohibiting that. Sometimes he'd have me lie down on the back floor board and close my eyes. Then he'd have me try to figure out how far he'd driven and how many turns he'd taken to see if I knew where we were. For a while I wanted to go into law enforcement and even took classes in the Police Explorers program during junior high. When my uncle wasn't working, he took me fishing or hunting, and when he later married and had the responsibilities of a family, he still managed to find some time for me. At the end of the day, though, I returned to my dysfunctional environment. Efforts by all of these good people fell short because my family life and neighborhood were so harsh that it overshadowed the good they extended to me. Still, these were all positive seeds planted in rocky soil. But I was still missing something, so my life continued to be one of turmoil with episodes of violence.

PART
THREE

MY
REFORMATION

Ephesians 4:22-24

"You were taught to put away your former way of life, your old self, corrupt and deluded by its lusts, and to be renewed in the spirit of y our minds and to clothe yourself with the new self."
(NRSV)

There is Light: Two Feet on the Right Path

In a hundred years I never thought my life would change so drastically in a parking lot. There was a dance club that was a college hangout where I would often go to hustle pool. The college guys were an easy target on the billiards table. I relied on the ol' pool player's trick of keeping the game even until the very end so my opponent was left wanting to play one more game to try to beat me. On this night I was by myself and had just parked my car when I saw two girls walking to a car which was parked right by mine. My attention was drawn to the pretty girl with long, brown hair, olive skin, and brown eyes. I found out later that the olive skin tone came from her Yugoslavian background. Neither of the girls was wearing a coat as they'd left them in the car. I came up with a quick pick-up line before they got in the car. "You know, it's people like you two who spread the flu around by not dressing properly." I directed the conversation to the cute girl and we exchanged banter for a minute. It was 9:30 p.m., I was just heading out for the night, and I wondered why they were leaving. It turns out they weren't much into the party scene and were already headed home. It was late fall with freezing temperatures at night so I said, "It's too cold to stand out here, but I think you're pretty. If you give me your phone number we can talk more and maybe get together and do something." She wrote down her name- Sandy- and phone number and drove off into the night while I went to make some spending money. I found out later that she knew who I was. She'd read about me in the newspaper when I'd wrestled and also recognized me from when I worked at the drive-in movie theater.

I did call Sandy shortly after we first met, and she invited me to her parents' house the following weekend. There was a raging snow storm going on, but I still went to her house. We talked for a long time, and Sandy made me tortilla chips with melted cheese on them. It was the first time I'd ever tried or heard of them. We began seeing each other often. Sandy was unlike any other girl I'd ever known. She had great character, morals, and manners. She was classy and intelligent. She was in college, had goals in life, and knew how to work hard to reach them. I respected these things right from the start, and because of my time with Randy Pascoe and other people who'd had positive influences on me, these values were no longer unfamiliar. I'd been growing discontented with the path I was on, and the desire to get back on the right road continued to grow the more time I spent with Sandy. I was awed by her constant patience and serenity. She was a Christian with a strong faith. We spent a lot of time together, and she invited me to go to church with her. One day she presented me with an Oxford Study Bible, and I began reading and studying the Christian beliefs. I don't know the particular moment when this happened, but at some point it was as if a light went on and, *wham,* this whole miracle of Christ hit me. Something moved in my soul. This light entered a part of me that had been dark. Some people said that's when the Holy Spirit came to me, but it seemed as though my mind was suddenly opened to the greatness of it all. For me, the feeling I had is summed up in the song *Amazing Grace* in the line that says, "How precious did that grace appear the hour I first believed." What astonished me is that I couldn't be humbled by bullies, bikers, judges, or jail, but the power of the scriptures stopped me in my tracks and put me in my place. I didn't instantly become a totally changed person, but I started noticing things that hadn't been there before, such as a feeling of calmness that I'd never experienced in the past. I still made some regrettable choices. To this day, I still have to focus and remind myself to do the right thing. However, I realized that I no longer felt like doing some of the things I'd been doing that had been getting me in trouble.

With Sandy, other parts of my life began to change, too. She introduced me to fine dining instead of the usual greasy burger spots. Take a bite. Put the spoon down. Talk. It took a little getting used to. She chuckled at the décor on the walls of my apartment: plastic replicas of dueling pistols glued onto a velvet backing, bracket cards from past wrestling tournaments, and a poster of Arnold Schwarzenegger. I expanded the category of movies I watched to include more than westerns and low budget drive-in movie flicks. One of the hardest changes was to change my environment and avoid the routine of hanging out in rough places with my old friends. I had to plan ahead and make a conscious effort to make sure I'd end up in a good place at the end of the day. Sandy and I continued to grow closer and on Valentine's

Day I took her to the best restaurant in town. Later that night I proposed. Well, I thought my idea for the proposal was perfectly satisfactory, but I got in trouble, anyway. I handed her the ring, since we'd already talked about getting married, and said with a smile, "Here's your ring." Sandy made me redo the proposal with a little more thought and enthusiasm. I still had a few rough edges.

We were married that summer. With Sandy's encouragement, I put a heavy emphasis back on college. I studied a lot. It seemed at times like every waking hour was study time. We didn't have much, and I needed a class that was only offered at a college three hours away. This was well before the days of online classes. To save money, I slept in the back of my vehicle for three weeks and would shower in the football field house. My new goals were focused on doing whatever it took to finish my education. I did graduate from college and was very proud of that since I didn't have any close relatives who'd reached that level of education. While I was in the process of finishing college, we were blessed with the birth of our son, Jordan, and two years later, our daughter Angela was born. My personal life was finally in order, I felt a peace that I had never before experienced, and I began attending church regularly.

Sandy, age 18, when we first met.

Our wedding day: August 3, 1984.

Sandy and I with our children, Jordan and Angela.

Career of Caring

With my fresh outlook on life, I developed new goals which I went after with all the intensity I'd learned from my coaches and from being in sports. In college I decided to become a teacher certified to work with special education students. Later, I earned my master's degree with an emphasis in behavioral disorders. My job has a 50% yearly turnover rate, yet I have stayed working with these challenging students for thirty years. By my request, I have asked to work with the most difficult students, those with conduct disorders, in the high school.

In many cases, these individuals are coming out of lock-up and trying to transition back into a public school. In many instances, it they aren't successful back in school, they will return to lock-up, so the stakes are high. Most of my students have been males, but I have worked with a few female students over the years. My childhood in that harsh environment has suited me well for this career since I work with many students who endure backgrounds similar to my own. Most of my students bond with me quickly. I let them know just enough about my childhood so they feel comfortable opening up to me. I always find a talent or strength area in each student I work with and help the student expand on this talent. It really boosts their self-esteem and increases their success rates. Their areas of talent have included athletics, art, music, cooking, welding, writing, and even being compassionate to some of our more severely physically and intellectually disabled special education students. Most of all, these difficult students I teach just want someone to give them attention and care about them.

There's no better example of this than a former student of mine who came to my program from Chicago to get away from the gang he'd joined. He had a couple of scars on his arms from when he'd been shot while in the gang. A hardcore, street-wise kid, he was tough and took no crap from anybody, but could also be very polite. One Friday afternoon, some of the students had earned enough good behavior points to watch a movie. The kids had been intently watching the movie for ten minutes while I did paperwork at my desk right next to them. A question from the group of kids broke my concentration. I looked up to find it came from the former gang member who said in a quiet voice, "Mr. Hamman, aren't you going to watch the movie with us?" I put my paperwork down and nodded. "Sure, I'll watch it with you." I moved a few feet from my desk to a chair closer to the TV where we proceeded to watch the show together. I realized at that moment how much it meant to some kids to just have the attention of an adult. After that, I always made sure the focus was on the students, and I let the paperwork wait.

So many of the students I've worked with haven't received the nurturing they've needed and deserved from adults in their life. I have had students in my program for all of their 9th-12th grade years, and in these four years, their parents did not come to one single school event. Not a conference, open house, career night, or any other school event. Even my own mother, who I know struggled emotionally, still tried to come to see me wrestle when she could. She encouraged me when I wanted to go to college, and with the little bit of money she had, she tried to help me out financially in order to do this. Now that I'm an adult, I can look back and see that she tried in the only ways she knew how. Some do have support, but so many of the students I work with have no one to love them or care about them. Our schools face an overwhelming task to fill the basic needs of students when those needs aren't being met at home. Consider this: whenever there is a teaching job available in our district, we have anywhere from 30-100 applicants for that position. These people have already proven themselves as college graduates. The hiring committee screens all of these applicants to interview the top four candidates. From there, they pick the best one. So it's no surprise that the teachers and principals I work with are top quality people. Our public schools and employees are put down a lot, but the real problem is a reflection of our society as a whole including the family structure. The teachers and coaches I have worked with have tried very hard to help young people become successful. During all my years as a wrestling coach, I not only tried to produce winning teams, but also to teach my wrestlers values to carry them through their lives. Even though my job has been difficult at times, it has been an incredibly rewarding career.

I'm also very proud of my family and the career paths they have chosen. Sandy is an elementary special education teacher, Jordan is a high school science teacher, and Angela is a middle school special education teacher.

One final note regarding my career; while growing up, my relatives were always telling me I was going to end up in prison, and I did. Before I got hired as a teacher, I needed a job and was hired as a state correctional officer and assigned to work in the prison. I worked there for one year before I landed my first teaching job. People may wonder how I could get hired as a state correctional officer or teacher after all the trouble I'd been in. Almost all my trouble involved fighting, which at the time was considered quite trivial. I was never convicted of a felony.

My uncle Allen in his police uniform. He spent time with me when he could, and I viewed him as my father. I always wished he was my dad.

Steve Joslyn and I have been close friends since junior high school. He always tried to be the voice of logic and reason.

I started channeling my weight lifting into something more productive than fighting. I was Mr. South Dakota in 1980. I would diet from 200 lbs. down to 165 lbs. for a contest.

My elementary P.E. teacher, Miss Jasper. She taught me how to set goals and work hard at a young age.

A newspaper clipping of me with the 50 lb. snapping turtle I caught when we were hunting turtles for food.

The poor little kid hunting small game (sparrow) in Norton-Froehlich.

Here I am, many years later, hunting big game in Africa.

PART
FOUR

MY
AWARENESS

Ecclesiastes 8:1

"Wisdom brightens a man's face and changes its hard appearance." (NIV)

Reflections

I don't blame my mom for everything bad that happened in my childhood. She did the best that she knew how. There were no talk shows or parenting blogs back then so she had to go by what she knew and saw others do. She suffered a lot of abuse herself, and her focus was probably on just trying to get through each day. Having lived through the Great Depression, she had grown up often wondering where the next meal would come from. So to my mom, a good parent was someone who provided food on the table and a home, and she set out to do just that. After she finally kicked my dad out of the house, he dropped me from his health insurance plan just out of spite and to make things more difficult for my mom. My mom had to work extra to pay for a private health insurance plan for me which meant she took on three jobs to keep the family afloat. She was a waitress and also a seamstress. When she wasn't working either of these jobs, she took in work out of our home doing alterations on clothes. She could sew just about anything and didn't even need a pattern to do it. To help out, I started working as a dishwasher in a restaurant when I was 13 years old. The main problem with all of this was that there was rarely a parent in the home so I was basically raising myself.

I found happiness in my life through commitment. Commitment to my family has been a top priority in my life. I'm committed to my job and the students I work with. I started a private business, and I'm committed to working hard at that, too. Commitment in all aspects of life is important if someone is going to be successful and happy.

I have been a strong advocate against bullying in the schools. I was the victim of bullying while growing up, and I also had a tendency to be a bully at times while growing up. In my work with students, I am constantly teaching them the harm that bullying can cause. I think the public schools are doing a good job trying to stop bullying as much as possible.

Teachers, coaches, and anyone who works with young people should never underestimate how important they may be in that child's life. It was the teachers and coaches in my life who helped plant the seeds to help me change into the person I am today.

To anyone who may read this and find these stories interesting, I also want them to understand that there were consequences in some way, to everything I did. My actions caused a lot of problems. I had a coach once tell me, "If you hang around a sewer you will smell like crap." That is true, and I was frequenting places that were bad environments, and it turned out to be crap. Put yourself in good environments, get as much education as you can, and work hard to reach goals because these are the greatest self-esteem builders there are.

Achievements happen for those who have the courage to overcome setbacks and personal conflicts. Those who set goals, have a plan to reach those goals, and work consistently will be successful.

Under the Influence is a fitting title for the story of my life. My life has been such a twisted trail that took so many different paths. I was once under the influence of my dysfunctional childhood, anger, and bad environments. I was under the influence of a wild peer group for a long time. Slowly, I came under the good influence of coaches, teachers, and sports programs. Then Sandy came into my life, and I was influenced by her. Most importantly, I came under the influence of Christianity. I hope that whoever reads this will judge me on who I am now, not who I once was. While telling the stories of my past, it was as if I was telling someone else's stories because now it doesn't even seem like I was ever a part of those events. So many of the people I grew up around died at a young age or are locked up. I am so grateful for the life I live now; the twisted path I was once on has become smooth and straight.

Where are They Now?

<u>Matthew:</u> Matt's shootout with the police did not occur. A criminal associate of Matt's had been arrested, unbeknownst to Matt, and in a plea agreement made a deal to set Matt up to be arrested. The associate arranged to meet with Matt, and when Matt showed up for the meeting, the police surprised him and made a quiet arrest. Matt was sent to the state penitentiary for the fourth time to be locked in that stone and steel cage from hell. Violence, corruption, sexual assaults, and every other form of bizarre human behavior occur inside these walls every day. The weak are preyed upon, and the strong survive. The powder 'women,' men taking on the look of women, flaunt and sell themselves for cigarettes or extra food. They powder their faces with white chalk from the weightlifting room. Using cherry juice, they stain their lips bright red, and also use the cherry juice to tint their underwear pink. They also cut their underwear into bikini-style panties. Everything and anything inside the walls can be used as a weapon: a sturdy piece of wire, a shard of plastic, or even a meat bone sharpened to a point. It was in this nightmare that the power of prayer changed Matt from the lost person he'd been.

I had written to Matt several times when he'd been incarcerated previously. I wrote to him about my change through Christ, let him know I was praying for him, and encouraged him to study the Bible. Matt's mother and others prayed for him, too, as they too believe there is great power in prayer. Through Christ, Matt made a complete change in his life. Miraculously, Matt was not charged as a habitual criminal. He had three separate felony charges on this fourth trip to prison. One was a 20-year charge, one was a 13-year, and one was a 5-year sentence charge. The state's attorney goes after the charge with the longest term and in a trial will charge you with that, or you can plead guilty and serve half of the longest term. So Matt should have served half of the 20-year sentence but for some unbelievable reason, the court date came and the paperwork for the 20-year sentence was lost. Then the state's attorney gave him the option of pleading guilty to the 13-year sentence and serving half the time, which he did, serving 6 ½ years. Matt believed it was divine intervention that led to this shorter sentence because that kind of paperwork *never* gets lost. It got him started thinking about faith and religion. Matt spent over 14 years of his life in lockup before he made this change. Today Matt has a loving wife and peace in his heart that he never knew. He is a devout Christian who attends church and reads the Bible often. I always expected Matt to be killed during criminal activity, killed by the police, or die of old age while locked up. None of us who knew Matt for so many years would have ever imagined things would have turned out like this for him. Matthew was in my wedding since I was married in between two of his prison stretches. I could not be more proud of him and happy for him. We still get together, but now it's to discuss philosophical issues.

Doug Wallin (Mr. I): He lives in Sioux Falls. He was in my wedding, and we are still close friends. He is married to a good, supportive woman, and they have raised three children who were successful athletes and are upstanding adults. Doug now has his temper under control, and is often the one telling others to calm down and do the right thing. I don't know where Doug stands as far as Christianity since he keeps a lot of things to himself, but when he's with Matt and me he listens when we discuss Christian views.

Alphonse Gerken (A Man of Bad Luck): Alphonse moved to western South Dakota and lives a peaceful life with his wife and family. Alphonse is a great role model for anyone facing hardships.

Steve Joslyn: He lives in Sioux Falls and is a businessman who travels internationally. I see Steve frequently, and we have long, philosophical talks. We still hunt together, and he still treats me like a brother. Steve remains a well-read and interesting person.

Randy Pascoe: This was my high school wrestling teammate who I looked up to and who gave me good advice. He joined the army and ended with a 20-year career in the military. After his military career, he became a state correctional officer working in Fort Leavenworth Military Prison. He is retired and living in Texas with his wife of 30 years. We correspond annually at Christmas time.

Randy Lewis: He is one of the greatest wrestlers that our country has ever produced, and he continues to stay active in the sport of wrestling by giving seminars on goal setting and motivation. He works with young people at wrestling clinics and is a great role model. He has moved back to Rapid City, SD where he is a business owner. We still keep in touch. I am honored that I had the opportunity to wrestle him in high school.

My mom: It still saddens me that my mom carried so much bitterness and unhappiness inside of her until the day she died of cancer in 2004. She was a heavy smoker, sometimes going through three packs a day. She was a wonderful cook and held many big family gatherings at her house over the years, complaining the whole time about being overworked yet seeming to enjoy every minute of it. She was happy when I was in sports and when I graduated from college. She also liked Sandy, loved all of her grandchildren, and spent time with all of them. Her distrust and negativity kept other people at bay, though.

My sisters: Both of my sisters have been waitresses over the years, like my mom was. One sister lives in California with her family. The other sister lives in the Sioux Falls area with her family.

Uncle Allen: He helped me in more ways than he ever knew. I appreciate everything he did for me. To this day, I'm an excellent shot and I attribute much of this to him taking me out shooting the .22 when I was young. He raised a good family and retired from the police force. A few years after retirement, he passed away due to a heart attack.

Judy Jasper: She was my grade school P.E. teacher who taught me how to set and achieve goals. She is retired and lives in Sioux Falls. I periodically have lunch with her when I'm in town. I have told her many times how she made a difference in my life. She recently donated a lot of money and time to a learning center east of Sioux Falls. Even in retirement, she has still found a way to keep educating young people.

Ray Wellman: My high school wrestling coach is also retired and living in Sioux Falls. He is indeed a coaching legend and even has a wrestling tournament named after him: The Ray Wellman Invitational. We get together often, and he knows how much he means to me. He told me that even though I had to be grabbed and disciplined many times for my behavior, he liked my aggressive style of wrestling. He said, "We just had to keep you from being kicked out of the sport."

<u>My dad (Smoe)</u>: He moved in with some other woman, and my mom finally divorced him. I refused to have contact with him as I got older as did both of my sisters. When I was getting good press for my wrestling accomplishments he would show up at tournaments to brag about being my dad. It was always about him. He died of brain cancer in 1993, and I didn't shed a tear. Only recently have I forgiven him and included him in my prayers. It's between him and God now.

Rainbow

When I was little, I often wished for a happy family. So when Jordan and Angela came along, I made a commitment for this to be different from them. I played with them, built forts, went on hikes, played hide-and-seek, listened to music, went sled riding, and played catch. I always attended their school and athletic events and arranged good vacations and hunting trips. They were indulged with various pets throughout their childhood. In the beginning of this book, I told a difficult story about a baby raccoon I'd wanted to raise. When my children were young, a co-worker found an abandoned baby raccoon. I brought it home and let Jordan and Angela bottle-feed it. We named it Rainbow, and she followed the kids all over the yard, usually ending up high in a tree. As soon as they were out of her sight, she'd start squealing and screaming and come running down from the tree. As she reached adulthood, it became clear that she needed to be with her kind. We brought her to a man who is an expert in re-releasing wild animals back into the wild. We loved Rainbow, so we set her free. A rainbow is a sign of love and hope and promises. Rainbow was a sign of love and hope that my children will remember a childhood of security, trust, and love.

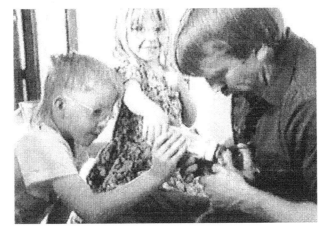

About the Author

Phil Hamman has been a teacher and coach for 30 years, spending most of that time teaching students with behavior disorders. He also co-teaches high school English. He has two children, Jordan and Angela, and lives with his wife Sandy in Sioux City, Iowa.

Made in the USA
Charleston, SC
09 April 2014